MEMPHIS BARBECUE

A SUCCULENT HISTORY OF SMOKE, SAUCE & SOUL

CRAIG DAVID MEEK

AMERICAN PALATE

Published by American Palate
A Division of The History Press
Charleston, SC 29403
www.historypress.net

Copyright © 2014 by Craig David Meek
All rights reserved

All photos by Craig David Meek unless otherwise noted.

First published 2014

Manufactured in the United States

ISBN 978.1.62619.534.9

Library of Congress CIP data applied for.

CONTENTS

Foreword, by Anna Mullins 5

Acknowledgements 7

Introduction 11

Chapter 1. The Early Days 17

Chapter 2. Electric Music 25

Chapter 3. Rapid Change 32

Chapter 4. Decline 45

Chapter 5. Moving East 50

Chapter 6. Revitalization 61

Chapter 7. Smokehouse 69

Chapter 8. Sole Survivors 75

Chapter 9. Competition 86

Chapter 10. Fame and Fortune 94

Chapter 11. Craftsmanship 104

Chapter 12. Hustle 119

Index 123

About the Author 128

FOREWORD

Memphis is, arguably, America's greatest city for barbecue. No city hosts as many stellar barbecue eateries as the Bluff City, and no other location offers the kind of variety found on Memphis menus. With restaurants in every neighborhood, feeding every demographic, Memphis proudly serves up unique barbecue on every corner. And while the affection for the Memphis staple is well known, the story behind the pitmasters is a tale deserving of a book.

One doesn't have to be a lover of barbecue to be interested in this book. Foodies will delight in the book's attention to culinary history—the traditions, ingredients and innovative approaches to established recipes are chronicled, lovingly, in the pages. Unlike many nods to southern cooking, barbecue is not treated as a kitschy backyard cuisine here but rather is given a powerful place in the canon of American regional food. Slow-cooked meats are a common language for food lovers, and this book makes the connections to other classic cooking methods. And if you happen to be a Memphis local or visiting tourist, Craig proves to be an experienced guide to answer the questions of where and what to eat. In a city with a multitude of delicious local places to choose from, this book serves as your docent to the options.

What really stands out about Craig's book is the examination of the food's context. Smoked pork wasn't made—or enjoyed—in a vacuum. The rich flavor and texture of the meat is the perfect metaphor for the landscape of the city and the food it fosters. With each restaurant he visits and each pitmaster he questions, Craig is keenly aware of not just the history of the business but also the socioeconomic complexities behind each dish. This is a city characterized by struggle and change, and the cuisine reflects that. The chapters reveal the relationship barbecue developed with the burgeoning music scenes, the interactions the restaurants and patrons had with local law and political power and the consequences of social forces on emerging businesses. As readers learn about the variations of slow-cooked pork shoulder and ribs, they will discover the stories and characters behind the barbecue pits, from the nationally known restaurants to the barrel cookers on street corners and in front of music clubs.

Anna Mullins
Executive Director, The Cotton Museum
Managing Editor, *High Ground News*

ACKNOWLEDGEMENTS

This book is the result of a lifetime of eating barbecue, nearly three years of blogging about it as a hobby and four months of intense interviewing, photographing, writing and editing before I suddenly found myself with a book contract and a deadline. Along the way, I received help from more people than I can list, but several stand out for their larger contributions.

First I have to thank my lovely wife, Jessica Elvert, for her understanding and encouragement as I battled with this project on nights and weekends while running a business. A shared love of food, music and travel are cornerstones of our relationship.

My commissioning editor from The History Press, Kirsten Schofield, offered me the opportunity to create this book and was a steady source of guidance, constructive criticism and helpful advice throughout its creation.

This book would not have been possible without all the people who took time from their busy schedules for interviews with me. They provided the cast of characters that brings this story to life. There are three people mentioned in this book whose contributions go far beyond the quotes attributed to them in the manuscript. Blake Marcum was my ambassador to the world of competition barbecue, providing countless valuable insights and introductions. Richard McFalls happily shared his encyclopedic knowledge of Memphis barbecue restaurant history along with photos he gathered while creating his always-fascinating "Memphis Barbecue Restaurants Ghost Pit Chronicles" blog. Blake and Richard both selflessly returned my constant calls, texts and e-mails loaded with esoteric barbecue questions, and both routinely went the extra mile to find the answers I needed. Beyond being an extremely talented barbecue cook, Brent McAfee is the definition of a friend, always willing to lend a hand at a moment's notice. Before I ever had a barbecue blog, I once approached him with questions about cooking two whole pigs in my backyard for my birthday. He immediately offered his services as pitmaster, and the end result was an epic feast. As a close friend and classically trained chef who has lived around the corner from us for years, he taught me and my wife a tremendous amount about the fundamentals of culinary technique.

Some of the best barbecue around Memphis is cooked by individuals in backyards. Travis Walker is a former coworker and longtime barbecue mentor whose homemade barbecue puts most restaurants to shame. He doesn't compete. He just does it for the satisfaction that comes from the endless pursuit of his own vision of perfection.

The history department on the fourth floor of the Central Memphis Library is a priceless asset for anyone researching any aspect of Memphis history. I am grateful to the entire ever-helpful and knowledgeable staff there, particularly Gina Cordell, the curator of the department's Memphis and Shelby County Room, who became my go-to source for all the seemingly random press clippings, photos and microfilm I needed to find. She never questioned my sanity at times when, while working on a book about barbecue, I suddenly wanted to see all the old newspaper reports I could find about something like Machine Gun Kelly's 1933 arrest in Memphis.

Newspapers publish the first drafts of history, and the old reports by the *Commercial Appeal* and the *Memphis Press Scimitar* were tremendous assets. In fact, the *Commercial Appeal* remains a tremendous asset today. I got numerous ideas for restaurants to visit from articles by food and entertainment writers Jennifer Biggs and Michael Donahue. The interviews with area restaurant owners conducted by the Southern Foodways Alliance, available online, were another huge advantage. All the quotes in this book are from interviews conducted by me unless specifically noted otherwise, but reading the Southern Foodways Alliance's interviews frequently provided useful background when I sat down with restaurant owners myself. Some of the quotes its members recorded were so perfect I had to include them, always providing credit where due.

Christian Brooks and Shade Sullins are the men behind the outstanding "Go Carnivore" blog, as well as good friends who share my love for the food and culture of the Dirty South. They have been steady accomplices in my exploration of the southern culinary world.

The inherent waste of build-and-abandon suburban sprawl has always disturbed me, but Strong Towns president Charles Marohn was the first person to fully articulate to me the complete measure of how destructive that approach to growth is and put real numbers into how self-defeating it is for our cities. His organization is based around the principle that "we can no longer simply disregard old investments in favor of new, but instead we need to focus on making better use of that which we are already committed to publicly maintain."

As this book was nearing completion, I called on two highly respected former teachers/professors to read over the manuscript and provide their thoughts. Nan Hackman and Dr. Cynthia Bond Hopson provided helpful input, along with some much-appreciated enthusiasm.

Finally, I owe a huge thank-you to my family, my mom and dad especially. My love for dry rub ribs and compulsive desire to understand how things work and how to improve them came from my dad. My love of books came from my mom, who always stressed the importance of me and my brother and sister being "seekers of knowledge."

INTRODUCTION

Memphis barbecue was such a constant presence in my early years that I never thought of it as a regional thing. Whenever people gathered to socialize, celebrate or mourn, there were always big aluminum trays of pulled pork, baked beans and cole slaw. If you were born and raised in Memphis, Tennessee, barbecue is just part of the fabric of life.

My dad was a loyal Jack's Bar-B-Q Rib Shack man up until the moment that restaurant sadly closed in 2013. Jack's is where I learned to love dry rub Memphis ribs. As a teenager in the '90s, I was working for a lawn crew that frequented local barbecue joints for lunch. During that time, the Three Little Pigs in East Memphis became my favorite stop for pulled pork sandwiches as I began to notice the variations in different barbecue that separated the great from the merely okay or the bad.

Since 2005, I've owned and operated a small wholesale automotive parts business that takes me all over the Mid-South for sales calls. It's a career that greatly deepened my love and respect for the people, history and culture of Memphis as I spent my days exploring it. But human beings are creatures of habit, and despite my travels, I tended to stick to a handful of longtime favorites when I was craving barbecue. One day, I encountered a problem at a common lunch stop from my lawn crew days.

When I worked in the suburb of Collierville, I usually stopped at Canale's Grocery at the intersection of Houston Hill and Raleigh-LaGrange to grab a ham sandwich. The little country store's owners cook their hams in a charcoal smoker for seven to eight hours, and the resulting meat is so flavorful that it is closer to good barbecue than the ham at most groceries. The sandwiches are made with store-bought bread, American cheese and mustard or mayo, with a chunk of iceberg lettuce and a tomato slice. The meat on them is good enough that none of that matters. It's sandwich perfection for a mere $2.50.

One day in the fall of 2011, I was walking up to the store when I saw a handwritten sign on the front that said, "No sandwiches today." I was disappointed, but I just hit up Collierville's Gus's Fried Chicken location for my southern food fix. Two weeks later, I was back at Canale's and was presented with an even worse sight: the store was locked up tight, with a sign that said, "Closed due to family illness."

Canale's thankfully reopened a few weeks later, but on the day I saw that sign, I was trying to think of a way to settle my craving for smoked pig when I remembered Captain John's Barbecue over on Highway 72. I remembered eating at Captain John's during the summer I interned at the *Collierville Herald* newspaper in 2000 while I was earning my journalism degree from the University of Memphis. Both the restaurant and the newspaper were located near the historic Collierville Town Square, where, coincidentally, I married my wife years later in 2007. (Our reception was at the Beethoven Club in Midtown. We served barbecue. A few years later, I celebrated one of my birthdays by cooking two whole pigs in my backyard. Like I said, barbecue is part of the fabric of life here.)

While enjoying a plate of pulled pork with beans, slaw and potato salad at Captain John's, I thought about just how many independent, locally owned barbecue places there are around Memphis; I see them everywhere while driving around for work. I made a quick Facebook post with my phone stating, "Despite a job that takes me all over the Greater Memphis Area, I've never made it a point to try every barbecue place in the area. Decided to remedy that starting today." From there I started trying a new barbecue place each workday for lunch. And each day, I'd post a few sentences about what I'd found.

Within two weeks, I decided that the daily posts would get annoying for friends who weren't deeply interested in barbecue. Meanwhile, I also wanted to write in more detail about the restaurants I was visiting and the neighborhoods where they were located. So I created the "Memphis Que" blog on September 26, 2011.

I didn't realize what I was getting into at first. I naïvely assumed that it would take a few months. In reality, after the first two months, I had about 40 posts and came to the realization that I had only scratched the surface.

Two years later, I was approaching 250 posts and had finally sampled most of the barbecue and soul food places in my work territory. But attempting to try them all is a steady game of Whack-a-Mole. There is always a new restaurant opening or a tip from a reader about some tucked-away spot, while other places fold in the crowded market. Memphis barbecue features a cast of characters too big to fit in one book, but just because a place isn't mentioned here doesn't mean it isn't worth checking out.

I kept the blog as anonymous as possible. I didn't want special treatment. I wanted to experience each restaurant as an average guy dropping by in a work van to grab lunch while delivering auto parts in the neighborhood. Plenty of the places I tried became regular stops, as I discovered that I could rely on affordable locally owned restaurants for lunch no matter what part of the Mid-South I was in.

A common question from my friends has been, "So where is the best place in town to eat barbecue?" The answer is that I can't even name the best place in the area within a few miles of my house; I have different favorite places for dry ribs, barbecue on a patio paired with local microbrews, a big sloppy pork sandwich, wet ribs and chicken, late-night ribs from a dive bar and chopped pork on top of a double cheeseburger. Memphis barbecue is art just like music or literature. You appreciate each work on its own merits. Asking me to name my favorite barbecue joint is like asking me to name my favorite book or song.

The correlation between barbecue and music extends even deeper in a city where the two are both defining elements of our culture. "What is Memphis barbecue?" is a question like "What is Memphis music?" Memphis music is blues, jazz, early rock-and-roll, soul, hip-hop, punk and garage rock. In a city filled with poverty, the defiant musical and culinary expression of the downtrodden created sounds and flavors that turned fortuitous musicians and restaurateurs into millionaires while influencing food and music across the globe.

This isn't a cookbook, but if you are serious about mastering the art of barbecue, there is a lot of advice you can glean from the talented pitmasters represented here. I've questioned everyone from world-famous restaurant owners and grand championship competition teams to tailgate enthusiasts and guys running roadside barbecue stands. I've eaten barbecue almost every day for several years.

Along the way, I've gotten a lot of advice about preparing barbecue. For example, always use pork shoulders. Also, avoid shoulders and cook Boston butts. Baby backs make the best ribs. No real barbecue joint would use baby backs; spare ribs are the way to go. The best flavor comes from cooking with straight charcoal. Or hardwoods like hickory and pecan. Or fruitwoods like apple and cherry. Or a combination of the three. Pork should go straight into the pit with no seasoning. Or it should be coated with a rub first. If you use a rub, it should contain plenty of salt to draw moisture out of the meat and create a marinade. Or it should contain very little salt, since it will dry the meat out. The most important secret is regularly basting the meat. Also, you shouldn't baste the meat because every time you open the pit doors, you interrupt the cooking process, letting out heat and moisture.

All those opposing views don't even delve into the epic debate over wet or dry ribs. There is no one definitive way to make Memphis barbecue anymore than one artist, like acoustic bluesman W.C. Handy, electric bluesman B.B. King, rock pioneer Elvis Presley, soul legend Isaac Hayes, garage rocker Jay Reatard or rapper Yo Gotti, could single-handedly define Memphis music. Part of the fun is exploring all the variations and learning to appreciate the best elements of each. There are some constants. Great music comes from hardship and struggle. Great barbecue is cooked slowly, over low temperatures, with plenty of natural smoke. But from there, a variety of cuts of meat, fuel sources, sauces and seasonings can all yield delicious results.

The tips you read in this book are all great advice, even if they completely contradict one another at times. What separates the expert artist from the novice is that they know exactly why they are doing what they are doing. They've made plenty of mistakes in the past and learned from them. They've honed techniques for creating the results they want—that express exactly where they came from.

When I started my quest, I quickly realized that I needed some sort of plan, both to make a fair comparison between the different restaurants and to avoid gaining one hundred pounds. I had recently seen Tom Naughton's myth-shattering documentary *Fat Head*, where he loses weight eating nothing but high-fat fast-food meals, so I followed his lead to create a simple set of rules. Every chance I got, I would stop at a barbecue place along my route and order pulled pork or ribs with beans and slaw. I tossed the bread that came with the meals. And I always ordered water for my drink. On the occasions that a place offered three sides, I got potato salad instead of fries. I kept my daily carbohydrate intake under one hundred grams, while I got the majority of my calories from natural animal fats. Although barbecue sauce can be loaded with sugar, I usually requested my sauce on the side so I could limit how much I used.

I still eat at barbecue and soul food restaurants almost every weekday for lunch, and I still follow those rules. At soul food restaurants, "vegetable" options always include items like macaroni and cheese, but I stick to real vegetables and legumes with my "meat and two sides" combos. I'm about twenty pounds lighter than I was three years ago, and my cholesterol ratios have improved dramatically. My friends call it my barbecue diet. I call it Dirty South paleo.

A large contingent of the restaurant owners I interviewed are over the age of seventy, still healthy and showing up before dawn every day to fire their pits up. So, the secret to a long life seems to be to find a career you are passionate about, work hard and eat a lot of barbecue.

CHAPTER 1
THE EARLY DAYS

There is no way of knowing exactly when our ancestors realized that hanging fresh meat in the smoke and heat of a fire helped preserve it while making it taste delicious, but the resulting flavor became hardwired into our DNA as something inherently satisfying and nourishing. It's the same ancient familiarity that draws humans to stare at a roaring fire. According to news reports, archaeologists recently unearthed a 300,000-year-old barbecue pit in an Israeli cave.

The culinary arts were one of the first human arts. Cave paintings followed as early humans invented the visual arts to pay tribute to the game animals that allowed us to evolve the large brains that define *Homo sapiens*, as author Lierre Keith noted in her book *The Vegetarian Myth*. After viewing the striking ancient renderings of game animals in the caves of southern France, a humbled Pablo Picasso famously remarked, "We have learned nothing new in twelve thousand years." Brains are largely made of fat and cholesterol. Hunting animals with primitive tools created a cycle that provided the raw materials for bigger brains to develop better tools to harvest more fat and cholesterol.

The earliest rub was salt, which helped preserve and flavor meat. There are still pitmasters today who only use salt, if anything, to season their meat before cooking, although many use additional seasonings like pepper, paprika and chili powder to pack additional punch into the delicious charred outer layer that barbecue enthusiasts refer to as bark. Good barbecue draws up ingrained nostalgia even in someone sampling it for the first time as it pushes primal buttons the eater didn't realize existed until their first bite.

Barbecue is generally cooked between 225 and 250 degrees with indirect heat from a nearby fire. Below that range, you are simply smoke curing. Above that range, you are grilling. In between, you have a sweet spot at which protein slowly absorbs the flavor and aroma of smoke while fat renders into a delicious liquid.

The slow time and low temperature break down fat and connective tissue. You can wrap a butt in foil and cook it in an oven at 250 degrees until it is done (internal temperature of about 195 degrees). The resulting meat will be tender and juicy, but it won't be barbecue. Real barbecue comes from meat absorbing smoke as it cooks. Smoke imparts a rich, complex flavor that ignites the most Paleolithic connections between the taste buds and the brain. As it penetrates the meat, smoke creates a telltale layer of pink coloration underneath the charred crust of bark called the smoke ring. The depth of the smoke ring is a good indicator of how much smoke flavor the meat absorbed.

There is also no way to find out when barbecue first appeared in Memphis, but pigs arrived with the first Europeans to see the area. Spanish explorer Hernando de Soto introduced the animals to America when he landed in Tampa Bay, Florida, in 1539 with thirteen pigs he brought along for food on the expedition. That small herd grew to number more than seven hundred pigs by the time of his death in 1542. The South was a perfect habitat for hogs, a fact that made them crucial to the sustenance of later inhabitants.

In 1540, De Soto and his troops passed through present-day South Carolina, where the newly introduced pigs met the traditional Native American practice of cooking meat with smoke and indirect heat to create what today's southerners recognize as barbecue. On May 8, 1541, De Soto reached the Mississippi River at a spot historians believe was just south of modern-day Memphis.

Memphis has been a major distribution hub since its early days. The steady movement of people and goods through the river-port city, which was founded in 1819 and incorporated in 1826, greatly influenced its rich heritage in both food and music. It is important for outsiders to understand that Memphis is not really a part of Tennessee, regardless of what any map says. Heading east from Memphis, you'll quickly encounter the hills of middle Tennessee followed by the mountains of east Tennessee. Memphis sits at the top of the alluvial plain commonly referred to as the Mississippi Delta. Its culture and geography is tied far closer to the flat, nutrient-rich river land of the Delta than it is to the rest of Tennessee.

Barbecue was frequently featured at picnics, parties and other social gatherings before restaurants offering it began to pop up. We will never know the identity of the first person to slow-cook a hog in a pit for his or her assembled friends and family. There is a good chance that no one at that inaugural gathering was able to read, much less document the occasion.

While Beale Street is lined with restaurants today, it was the city's main distribution center from the 1840s through the 1920s, according to Performa Entertainment president John Elkington in his book *Beale Street: Resurrection of the Home of the Blues*. As the Civil War began, Memphis "was a bustling frontier town with a population of 8,900," according to the book *Looking Up at Down: The Emergence of Blues Culture* by William Barlow. As the first major Southern city to fall to the Union—in a brief river battle that left the city mostly unscathed—Memphis, Elkington wrote, received a huge influx of black citizens fleeing other parts of the South during the Civil War, turning Beale Street into an influential center for black culture and a major force in the development of the blues in the early decades of the twentieth century.

By the 1870s, the population had grown to around 50,000 people before a series of yellow fever epidemics killed more than 5,000 people and caused about another 25,000 to flee. The fever was spread by mosquitoes, which thrived in the city's notoriously filthy environment at the time. "There was no city sewer system. Water was collected in cisterns, and maimed animals were left rotting in Downtown streets made of ill-advised cypress paving blocks that rotted and caved in, creating chasms that broke the legs of horses and mules," according to a September 11, 2010 *Commercial Appeal* article on the epidemic. "Memphis began to recover quickly after 1878. Its artesian water supply was discovered and turned into one of the purest water supplies in the nation in the 1880s. Its charter was restored. Its sanitation and sewer systems became models for other cities." By 1900, the population had reached 100,000, and between 1900 and 1950, it nearly quadrupled from 102,350 to 396,000 residents.

Alcohol prohibition became Tennessee state law in 1909 but was largely ignored in Memphis, especially the area around Beale Street that became a red-light district, filled with prostitution, gambling, drinking and drugs, according to Barlow. "Moonshine liquor and marijuana were sold in the saloons and on the street corners up and down Beale Street. Cocaine was sold in neighborhood drugstores; a small boxful cost five or ten cents," he wrote. "It's use as a stimulant had long been encouraged among black laborers by white employers…It was estimated by the police at the turn of the century that up to 80 percent of the black workforce in the city used cocaine."

Beale Street in the 1910s. *Courtesy of the Memphis and Shelby County Room, Memphis Public Library.*

In the early '20s, as Beale was at its rowdiest, barbecue began appearing in restaurants around the Mid-South. Bozo's Hot Pit Bar-B-Q on Highway 70 in nearby Mason, Tennessee, opened in 1923. Still in operation, it is enough of a time capsule that part of the 2005 Johnny Cash biopic *Walk the Line* was filmed there. Abe's Bar-B-Q in Clarksdale, Mississippi, has a history dating back to 1924, when Lebanese founder Abe Davis opened it as the Bungalow Inn, according to *BBQ Joints: Stories and Secret Recipes from the Barbeque Belt* by David Gelin. In 1937, Abe Davis changed the name to the Delta Inn when he moved to the legendary Crossroads at Highways 61 and 49, where legend says bluesman Robert Johnson sold his soul to the devil in exchange for his musical prowess. In 1960, Abe's son, Pat Davis, changed the restaurant's name yet again in honor of his father.

In 1922, Leonard Heuberger, whose German parents owned a Front Street saloon while he was growing up, opened a small seven-stool hamburger stand called Leonard's Lunch at the corner of Trigg and Latham in South Memphis. It transitioned into the Leonard's Pit Barbecue people know and love today when Heuberger relocated to the nearby corner of Bellevue and McLemore in 1932. He traded a Model A Ford for the property, which was a grocery store that he converted into a restaurant, according to grandson Bill Hughes. Heuberger learned to make barbecue from a black woman who was the previous owner of the site and whose name has been lost to history.

Memphis barbecue legend John Willingham credited the now universal Memphis-area practice of serving cole slaw on barbecue sandwiches to Leonard's in his 1996 book *John Willingham's World Champion Bar-B-Q*, stating that "it was used to 'stretch' the meat one afternoon at Leonard's BBQ, when supplies ran low. Need I mention the combination was an instant success?"

Cole slaw can range from the sharp and tangy Leonard's-style rendition, which is dominated by mustard and vinegar, to sweet and creamy versions centered on mayo and sugar. The dish came to the United States with Dutch immigrants. *Koolsalade* is the literal Dutch term for cabbage salad, a dish of cabbage dressed with vinegar, eggs and spices that dates back to Roman times. *Koolsla*, as the name was shortened to, has been in the United States since colonial times and evolved into the Americanized cole slaw variations we know today.

While Leonard's now offers outstanding barbecue ribs along with southern staples like fried chicken and catfish, it was just a sandwich shop in its early days. The pork sandwich is still the most common form of barbecue in Memphis, and this is what Memphians are referring to when they talk about getting "a barbecue." Somewhat confusingly, sandwich meat almost always comes from the shoulder of a pig whether it is from a "shoulder" or a "butt." The meat from the lower part of the shoulder is called a "picnic shoulder," or just "shoulder" for short, while the meat from the leaner upper part of the shoulder, which is usually sold without skin, is counterintuitively called a "Boston butt." The real butt area of a pig is generally used for ham. In barbecue restaurants, the word "butt" is shorthand for the Boston butt cut of a shoulder.

Leonard's still makes sandwich meat with the classic picnic shoulders. The Bellevue location closed in 1991 but is still remembered for its large drive-in area that accompanied the dine-in restaurant. Heuberger picked up the drive-in concept from Fortune's Jungle Garden—a Memphis restaurant that opened at Union and Belvedere in 1921 and is credited as the first drive-in in the United States—after he got in trouble with the police for selling beer from his restaurant's walk-up sales window and hired carhops. Serving an open beer to someone on foot was forbidden at the time, but apparently drinking behind the wheel of a car was no big deal.

As a hard-partying river-port town in the Bible Belt, throughout the city's history Memphis residents have frequently acted ashamed of its booze-soaked culture rather than embracing it like New Orleans. Hughes recalls a

Customers pile into the drive-in at Leonard's Barbecue at Bellevue and McLemore during the early 1950s. *Courtesy of Richard McFalls by way of Tommy Leonard Hughes.*

SERVING REAL • • • • • • • • • •

HOT **PIT BARBECUE** OFF THE PIT

IN MEMPHIS FOR OVER 33 YEARS

ORIGINATORS OF

MR. BROWN PIG & MISS WHITE PIG

The Barbecue Bean Pot & the Half & Half Plate

Custom Barbecuing for Picnics & Parties   (½ Spaghetti & ½ Barbecue)

Drive-Inn Parking Service

Air Conditioned Dining Room

Call WHitehall 2-4010

IN BUSINESS SINCE 1922
1140 S. BELLEVUE BLVD.

LEONARD'S
PIT BARBECUE

(McLEMORE AT BELLEVUE)

A 1955 advertisement for Leonard's Barbecue. *Courtesy of Richard McFalls.*

female customer at Leonard's who always wanted a beer with her barbecue after church. But that beer had to be brought to her in an iced tea glass with a spoon in it, wrapped in a napkin and dressed with a lemon slice to disguise it from her church friends.

Hughes's mother, Thelma, was born in 1923 and literally grew up in the restaurant. Leonard and his wife, Edith, lived in the restaurant at Trigg and Latham, and behind the one located at Bellevue and McLemore. Thelma was sixteen when her parents finally bought a house in 1939.

In a 1979 interview with the *Commercial Appeal*, Thelma Hughes said that as a little girl she enjoyed visiting with customers in the restaurant and mentioned a nicely dressed gentleman "who sat next to her one night and struck up a conversation. He asked her if he could eat dinner with her every night. She was delighted. 'Then after about two weeks, one night he didn't show up and I was heartbroken. The next day my daddy took me aside and told me the man wouldn't be back. "You don't mean he's dead, do you?" I asked. He said "no" but that he was in jail. I found out it was Machine Gun Kelly,'" she said referring to famed Prohibition-era gangster George "Machine Gun Kelly" Barnes, who was arrested in Memphis by Federal Bureau of Investigation agents on September 26, 1933, when Hughes was ten years old. Barnes was hiding at a house around the corner from Leonard's at 1408 Rayner Street while on the run from Oklahoma City. His return to Oklahoma marked the first time in U.S. history that a defendant was transported by airplane. He was convicted and sent to Alcatraz.

Alongside Leonard's, there was another barbecue hangout spot where crowds of Memphians congregated from the '30s through the '60s. During her 1979 interview, Thelma Hughes, said, "While I was dating, I was the only one who didn't go to Leonard's because all the carhops and everybody knew me. I hung out at the Pig-N-Whistle."

The Pig-N-Whistle opened in an English Tudor-style building at 1579 Union in 1929. Old tavern signs in England commonly displayed a pig and a whistle as a sign that it was a place to eat and "wet your whistle" back in an era when many people were illiterate, according to current owner Bill Rupert. The restaurant quickly became so popular that carhops began waiting on the curb to jump onto the running boards of vehicles as they pulled in to take down orders and then ran them out to customers who didn't want to wait to get into the building.

"It was a real hangout. That's where Memphis went to let its hair down," said longtime manager Joe Richey during an interview with the *Commercial Appeal* published on November 10, 1994. The original Union location closed in 1966. There were other locations throughout the Memphis area over the years, but only the one owned by Bill Rupert in the Kerrville community just north of Millington remains today.

Rupert never witnessed the bustling '50s era of the Union Avenue Pig-N-Whistle, but he still hears stories about it from customers. The fond memories people associate with the name and the Old English logo are both a blessing and a curse for the brand's caretaker. "From a marketing standpoint, you don't want a name with so many syllables and that is so hard to read, but it means a lot. When we do catering in other areas, we have people get angry, and I mean really genuinely angry, that we don't have a place near them anymore."

The ties to the past also flavor the sauce—a classic Memphis-style combination of molasses, vinegar and tomato with hints of paprika and cumin. "I'm happy with it. I've never wanted to change it," Rupert said. The molasses provides a far more subtle sweetness than the many high fructose corn syrup–dominated sauces on the market today.

CHAPTER 2
ELECTRIC MUSIC

By the 1950s, barbecue was so common in Memphis that it could put a familiar face on new foods. Horest Coletta was just six months old when his parents immigrated to the United States from Viticuso, Italy, in 1918. In 1922, his parents, Emil and Candida, opened a drive-in on South Parkway that mainly served ice cream, along with Italian foods like ravioli. Horest was running the restaurant in the mid-'50s when service members from the Memphis Naval Air Station in Millington began requesting pizza, which they encountered while serving in Italy.

"My dad went to Chicago to learn how to make pizza," said Horest's son, Jerry Coletta, who owns the restaurant today. Local diners eyed the traditional Italian pies with suspicion. "It wasn't going over very well. People had never heard of pizza, and they were hesitant to try it," Jerry said. So, his father put a barbecue pit in the restaurant's basement and began topping his pies with a thick layer of shoulder meat since "everyone in Memphis was familiar with barbecue."

At Coletta's, barbecue pizza starts life as an ordinary cheese pizza. To avoid drying out the barbecue in the intense heat of the pizza oven, the restaurant completely cooks the pies before the already-hot shoulder meat and tomato-based homemade barbecue sauce are added just before serving.

While '50s-era Memphians were initially skeptical of pizza, they quickly embraced the barbecue version. Elvis Presley loved them. The back room he always requested is still designated the "Elvis Room" and is heavily decorated with Elvis memorabilia. Although Presley came by on occasion, it was far more common for him to send his wife, Priscilla, to pick up a stack of pizzas, which sold for $1.75 apiece at the time, to take back to Graceland. She had a charge account with the restaurant and came by several times per week. Fans know that the back room was where Presley sat when he was in the building, and Jerry said that he starts getting calls from around the world to reserve tables there nine to ten months before the annual Elvis Week in August that commemorates the singer's death.

By the time Presley was eating barbecue pizza at Coletta's, the Memphis music scene had changed dramatically from the piano-based acoustic blues that dominated Beale Street before World War II, when W.C. Handy lived there and it earned its nickname as "the home of the blues." While Memphis was hit hard by the Depression, the vice corridor along Beale initially continued to thrive, according to Barlow. "One saloon keeper financed a free soup kitchen with the profits from liquor and games of chance," he wrote.

Ironically, the drinking and partying came to a halt with the end of state prohibition in 1939, according to Laurie B. Green in her book *Battling the Plantation Mentality: Memphis and the Black Freedom Struggle*. Former Memphis mayor "Boss" E.H. Crump directed public safety commissioner Joseph Boyle to "clean up" Beale when he realized that legalized alcohol would eliminate a formerly lucrative source of funds at a time when the senate was investigating the Crump organization's reliance on payment's from the "underworld."

Crump was no longer mayor but still had near complete control of the city at the time. He was elected mayor in 1909 and only served until 1916, when the Tennessee legislature forced him out of office for violating the state's prohibition law with his lucrative ties to illegal alcohol establishments, Green noted. He briefly served as mayor again in 1940, but from 1916 until his death in 1954, his powerful political machine controlled the city and effectively picked every mayor who served during that period.

When Crump decided to crack down on Beale, the police began an immediate campaign of harassment against black business owners who resisted the Crump machine. "In Mid-November [1940], Boyle announced intentions to clear the city of 'undesirables' and launched a series of raids on cafés and saloons on Beale Street and in other black neighborhoods," wrote Green. "In December, Boyle made clear that the city would be a hostile place for black migrants who did not want to do agricultural labor."

During the segregated years of the mid-twentieth century, white people shopped and ate on Main Street, while Beale served as the "Main Street" for black Memphis. Green quoted black Memphian Elaine Lee Turner, who said,

Beale Street in the 1940s. *Courtesy of the Memphis and Shelby County Room, Memphis Public Library.*

"Beale Street was a street where black people congregated, and you could go in any building, any business and you were treated like a first-class citizen. You were at home on Beale Street…And when you turned that corner, going on Main Street, then you had just a whole different atmosphere…When you went on Main Street, you had to be on guard."

Segregation wasn't a completely two-way street. White Memphians like Presley spent time on Beale absorbing the music and fashions. During the '50s, Beale Street was only home to a few music venues, and those venues mostly focused on jazz and variety shows, said Dale Franklin, a local music expert and KWEM radio consultant for the Mid-South Community College in West Memphis, Arkansas. A 10:00 p.m. curfew for black residents and noise ordinances that closed music venues at midnight left revelers heading over the bridge to the wide-open world of juke joints and gambling along Broadway in West Memphis during the post–World War II blues period, when the electric guitar fundamentally altered the music's sound. "West Memphis was the red-light district for Memphis. It was just wide open over there. There was a juke joint on every corner. The future of Memphis music was right there," Franklin said.

As the electric sound of the postwar period gave birth to rock-and-roll, artists like B.B. King, Muddy Waters and Howlin' Wolf honed their skills in West Memphis playing fish fries, barbecues and baseball games—anywhere that they could find an audience. It was a period when Beale Street was mainly home to clothing stores, groceries, drugstores and pawnshops. It had just two music clubs, while there were thirty-five to forty in West Memphis, Franklin said. In an era before modern zoning laws, most of the juke joints were houses serving as do-it-yourself clubs. They had music in the front, gambling in the back, plenty of liquor everywhere and possibly food for sale as well.

"Almost all those clubs had gambling. In the late '60s, they stopped that. The FBI came in and closed them up," said William's Bar-B-Q owner William Maxwell. His restaurant on 14th Street in West Memphis is an old-fashioned barbecue joint in a ramshackle little building in the middle of a neighborhood where southern music developed into a force that influenced the rest of the world.

The boardinghouse where Howlin' Wolf stayed is on 11th Street, three blocks over from where William's is located now. The towering bluesman, whose real name was Chester Arthur Burnett, had a radio show at the KWEM station, which was located at 2nd and Broadway. B.B. King played nightly at Miss Annie's Diner on 17th Street, where he could make twelve dollars per night compared to the twenty per week that was the prevailing wage on a cotton farm at the time, according to Franklin.

In 1961, Maxwell was fixing shoes at the Main Shoe Shop in West Memphis. As a sign of how loose codes and regulations were in that time, the shoe store began selling his barbecue in 1963 as well. In 1969, he opened his own barbecue joint on 8th Street when it was home to a heavy concentration of blues clubs. The seventy-seven-year-old saw performances by B.B. King and Albert King in the neighborhood, which never went to sleep in that era. "They was partying all night," he said. "We had something didn't no one else in Memphis have. They'd stay up all night and dance and party, but there wasn't any killing like there is now. People would fight and be friends again the next day." The busiest days for the clubs were Sundays, when blue laws shut Memphis down.

Maxwell paid rent on the 8th Street location for three decades before buying his current 14th Street building and relocating there in 1998. He still cooks in the old steel charcoal pit that he moved with him. William's sells massive barbecue sandwiches and not much else besides burgers and smoked sausages. "If you sell too many things, you've got too much waste," Maxwell explained. "Ribs and chicken wings; those are two things I don't fool with."

The restaurant doesn't have many places to sit. In fact there are as many nonfunctional old televisions cluttered along an unused counter as there are tables. Most of the business comes from carryout customers. A barbecue

Former boardinghouse on 11th Street in West Memphis, Arkansas, that was home to legendary blues musician Chester Arthur Burnett, known to the world as Howlin' Wolf.

sandwich at William's and some time spent looking at empty juke joints around it provide a glimpse back into the real world of the blues, away from the neon lights and tourists of downtown Memphis in an area where the patina is completely real and totally unvarnished.

Maxwell makes his sauce, slaw and beans from scratch. He uses Boston butts instead of shoulders, explaining that "a shoulder has too much waste." People who enjoyed his barbecue as children bring their grandkids to eat it today. But the volume of business has declined with the neighborhood around the restaurant, where abandoned and burned-down buildings are a common sight. "It's dead. There's not a lot of money over here. There's lots of empty buildings. If I had to pay rent, I'd be gone. I'm going to stay as long as I can make enough to pay them," he said motioning to the employees working in the kitchen behind him. "I'm okay. I don't need much. I'm a poor man."

The aging former main strip next to the restaurant was once the city's retail and nightlife center. Its old buildings possess enough character to make it easy to look past the blight and daydream about how it could look in a revitalized state. Most of the town's retail business shifted over to the interstate access road, where a Super Walmart is located, in a scenario that has played out in countless cities throughout the country in recent decades as municipalities have mistaken a debt-driven build-and-abandon pattern of waste for economic growth.

Walking around Broadway in West Memphis today, it is hard to believe that an area with such a rich musical history could sit so forgotten ten minutes from downtown Memphis, even though Memphis institutions like Sun Studio, Beale Street and Stax Records all experienced similar neglect before their eventual resurrections. "We are in 1977, when Sun Studio was empty, nobody knew who Sam Phillips was and the city was fixin' to tear Beale Street down," Franklin said of the decaying, history-drenched neighborhood that surrounds William's Bar-B-Q. The old KWEM radio station on Broadway at 2nd is long gone, replaced by a Regions Bank branch. "That was the most important radio station in music history, but most people haven't heard of it. KWEM radio was like the back door to Sun Studio," he noted. It went on the air in 1947.

KWEM followed in the footsteps of Memphis-based WDIA radio as advertisers began to recognize the value of marketing to black consumers. Trying to compete with the entertainment upstart of television, WDIA hired its first black disc jockey, Nat D. Williams, in 1948, according to music scholar David Whiteis in his book *Southern Soul-Blues*. By the end of the following year, WDIA had an all-black format that was a huge success. During the same period, the success of the *King Biscuit Time* radio show on KFFA in Helena, Arkansas, lead to "Sonny Boy" Williamson being pictured on bags of King Biscuit cornmeal, Franklin said. Both KWEM and WDIA allowed performers to pay for on-air playing time.

"They were colorblind," Franklin said. For talented musicians, buying a short block of playing time on the radio was an investment that paid for itself in increased turnouts at live performances. Elvis Presley played on KWEM a year before cutting the groundbreaking "That's All Right" single in Memphis at Sun in 1954. "What rock-and-roll really was was the desegregation of American music," Franklin said.

Sun Studio founder Sam Phillips worked at the easy-listening WREC radio station at the Peabody Hotel in Memphis but was personally a huge fan of the blues. Phillips loved radio and listened to stations like KWEM and WDIA to find new talent, said Sun Studio public relations director Jayne Ellen Brooks. His enthusiasm for the raw new sounds developing around him, combined with his willingness to record both black and white artists, led to Phillips capturing early rock-and-roll milestones like Ike Turner's 1951 hit "Rocket 88" and Presley's "That's All Right," along with the original recordings of West Memphis juke joint regulars like B.B. King and Howlin' Wolf.

Barbecue

Barbecue Cafe No 1
   For White Patrons
      115 Vance Av ------------------------5-9643
   For Colored Patrons
      115 Vance Av ------------------------5-9643
Barbecue Cafe No 2
   For White Patrons
      799 S Main --------------WHitehl 2-9227
   For Colored Patrons
      799 S Main -----------WHitehl 6-9208

Number 115 Vance is most famously known as the former home of Raiford's Hollywood Disco, a nightclub with prominent "No discrimination" signs where crowds of black and white patrons would dance and drink together into the early morning hours. It was renamed Hollywood Disco when Robert Raiford moved to Paula & Raiford's Disco on 2nd Street in 2007 after three decades at the Vance location. In 1955, it was a barbecue café during the era of segregation. *Courtesy of Richard McFalls.*

After Phillips left the original Sun location in 1960 to open Phillips Recording around the corner, the building sat empty for years, during a period when nearby Beale Street declined to a crumbling, nearly completely abandoned state. Radio host Gary Handy bought the Sun building in 1985 and reopened it as a recording studio and tourist attraction. Jim Schorr bought it shortly after as the revitalization of Beale Street was gaining momentum, Brooks said. His son, John Schorr, gathered the memorabilia to create the studio's upstairs museum, starting in 2001, and had the site designated a National Historic Landmark in 2003.

CHAPTER 3
RAPID CHANGE

Today, dry rub ribs are a signature element of Memphis barbecue. But up through the 1960s, the Memphis barbecue scene was entirely dominated by sandwich shops. Greek restaurant owner Charles Vergos created dry rub ribs at the Rendezvous in 1964. The size and price of shoulders makes them far more economical than ribs. The relatively thin and fatty rib meat takes more skill to cook correctly, but in the hands of an expert pitmaster, they justify the extra hassle and expense with a delicious flavor that even the best shoulder meat can't compete with. Smoke can only penetrate so far into a shoulder, while ribs can be "pink to the bone."

The Rendezvous' history—as pieced together from June 11, 1989 and February 23, 1991 retrospectives published in the *Commercial Appeal*—began in 1948 when twenty-two-year-old Vergos teamed with a partner to open a tavern called Wimpy's in an alley off Union, by where the One Commerce Square building is today. When the partnership fell apart in 1953, Vergos set up shop in the building's basement and christened it the Rendezvous. The tucked-away location was popular with businessmen taking the afternoon off, Peabody guests, area disc jockeys and men relaxing while their wives shopped on Main Street.

The Rendezvous was a beer joint serving sandwiches and cheese plates until Vergos converted an old coal chute in the basement to a charcoal pit in 1964. According to the 1989 *Commercial Appeal* article, Vergos remembered walking through downtown Memphis as a child and seeing black families cooking pork over hot coals in washtubs in their yards. "That's the original barbecue. Black people invented barbecue," the paper quoted Vergos. "White people just capitalized on it."

At the time, ribs were a cheap, unpopular cut of meat. To season them, Vergos combined traditional Greek flavors like salt, pepper, garlic and oregano with the cayenne pepper, chili powder and paprika that he'd become fascinated with after encountering them in Cajun cuisine in New Orleans.

Vergos always rejected the "dry rib" name. "I never called them that. People tacked that name on because they weren't messy like regular barbecue," he told the *Commercial Appeal* in 1991. The Rendezvous rub is the original Memphis rendition, and the spacious old basement, crowded with aging memorabilia, provides a timeless atmosphere. But people looking to experience great Memphis barbecue have to understand that the ribs at the Rendezvous aren't barbecue and don't claim to be. Cooked roughly eighteen inches over a bed of charcoal for about an hour, the Rendezvous serves seasoned and chargrilled ribs. They still taste good, but more like a grilled pork chop dusted with dry rub than barbecue. The Rendezvous put a Greek spin on charcoal-cooked pork, and local barbecue cooks adopted the seasoning approach for their own meats. A rib cooked for one hour at a temperature over 400 degrees is a completely different category of food from a rib cooked for four hours at 250 degrees. But the dry rub seasoning altered the face of Memphis barbecue during a period of massive change for the city.

During the '60s, Beale Street entered a period of steady decline that culminated in a disastrous urban renewal plan invoked by the Memphis Housing Authority in 1968, according to John Elkington. It was an era when "urban renewal" was an Orwellian term for governments taking over and bulldozing large stretches of properties. The City of Memphis owned all of Beale Street from 2nd to 4th Street, with the exception of the A. Schwab dry goods building, and the City Council nearly approved bulldozing the entire area in the late '70s. "The city had lost focus on where it wanted to go and how it planned to get there," Elkington wrote of an era when "the Peabody Hotel closed and was sold on the courthouse steps in 1974."

In 1968, construction of the One Commerce Square tower at the original Rendezvous site caused the restaurant to relocate to its current location in an alley off Union across the street from the Peabody Hotel. On May 18, 1976, the Rendezvous was heavily damaged by a two-alarm fire that began around 5:00 a.m., according to a *Commercial Appeal* story from the following day. While pit fires are the bane of charcoal-pit restaurants, the Rendezvous fire was caused by an electrical short in an area between the false ceiling of

An increasingly vacant and blighted Beale Street in 1976. *Courtesy of the Memphis and Shelby County Room, Memphis Public Library.*

the restaurant and the ground floor above it, according to Department Fire Marshall Charles Means in the *Commercial Appeal* story. The paper reported that the only casualty of the fire was the restaurant's beloved pet parrot, Clyde, while a turtle that was an eight-year inhabitant of the restaurant was rescued during the salvage operation.

Vergos told the paper, "It's bad but we'll survive it. You just have to look at it and go back again. As far as we're concerned, we'll be open as soon as we can get that water and smoke out of there." It was a prophetic statement from the tenacious owner despite quotes from firemen that water was eighteen inches deep in the basement restaurant. On May 25, 1976, the *Commercial Appeal* reported that the Rendezvous had already reopened.

"The Memphis Fire Department had barely finished pumping the water out of the basement when Vergos, no stranger to hard work, and his staff of 32 began their cleanup and salvage operation," the paper reported. The city's close-knit Greek community, led by Reverend Nicholas L. Vieron of the Annunciation Greek Orthodox Church, "rolled up their sleeves and went to work" to help Vergos.

"It makes you feel real good," Vergos said. He was luckier than his upstairs neighbor. Famed local steakhouse Jim's Place, which is now located in East Memphis, suffered extensive damage that required two months of repair work, according to the paper.

The Rendezvous is the kind of institution that develops over decades, overseen by a big personality, never really changing. Vergos was known as a large and loud man who cussed constantly but always maintained a worn but clean establishment. He didn't tolerate foolishness from customers.

In a 2008 interview with the Southern Foodways Alliance, one of his sons, John Vergos, recalled the first time the Rolling Stones visited the restaurant:

> *The Rolling Stones were a pretty raggedly looking group and so they were on the first tour of Memphis and they were at the Peabody Hotel. And so they came down to the Rendezvous and my father was on the verge of throwing them out and was kind of rude to them at first, and then all of the sudden they got a call from the manager at the Peabody that said "Charlie, Charlie." He said the Rolling Stones are coming down there and he made some comment—he said are you talking about those shaggy-ass looking—I'm going to throw them. He said "No, no, Charlie; don't." He probably used more expletives than that. And so he said something to them. He said, "I ought to throw you out but the guy at the Peabody said y'all know how to play some music," or something along those lines. And they still come—every time they've toured the United States they always come to the Rendezvous.*

In the same interview, John Vergos summed up the unique character that separates Memphis from the rest of Tennessee: "As a matter of fact, contrasting Memphis and Nashville, Memphis has a strong Jewish community, strong Lebanese community; you know Nashville is just kind of white bread and, and I just think that you know Memphis just has kind of a rowdiness. It appeals to me as a city. New Orleans has many of the same factors."

As the Rendezvous was building a name for itself in the '60s, two new chains were busy creating a tremendous amount of barbecue infrastructure, which still serves as the basis for many of the independent restaurants around Memphis. Loeb's Bar-B-Q and Coleman's Bar-B-Q both started in the '60s, and both fell apart after expanding too fast in attempts to dominate the Memphis barbecue market. They left behind a large number of buildings equipped with old-fashioned brick-and-steel charcoal pits. Some are still empty; some have been converted to other uses, ranging from thrift shops to convenience stores; and some have been reborn as mom and pop barbecue joints.

Richard McFalls refers to the dormant pits with their distinctive brick chimneys as "ghost pits." He photographs the old restaurant sites for his "Memphis Barbecue Restaurant Ghost Pit Chronicles" blog, where he details the buildings' locations, conditions and current uses. It's a hobby for McFalls, age sixty-two, a Chattanooga native who has worked as a copy editor at the *Commercial Appeal* for the past thirty-four years. He scours old phone books, city directories and microfilm newspaper archives in his quest to track down all the city's forgotten pits, and his blog is a treasure-trove of Memphis barbecue trivia.

Former Loeb's locations around town include the Three Little Pigs, Bryant's Breakfast on Summer Avenue and the Boss Man Pit Stop on Getwell. Old Coleman's locations serve as Captain John's in Collierville, Moma's Bar-B-Q in Bartlett, Tastee Bar-B-Q on Brooks Road, Reese's Bar-B-Q on Winchester, Smokin D's Pit Stop in Millington, Showboat Barbecue on Hickory Hill Road and the three remaining Coleman's sites (Millbranch; Hernando, Mississippi; and Senatobia, Mississippi).

Showboat's seventy-nine-year-old owner, Porter Moss, witnessed the rise and fall of both chains firsthand. He began his barbecue career in the late '50s, when he and coworker A.B. Coleman left the Montesi's grocery store on Summer Avenue to work at the Tops Bar-B-Q across the street. The first Tops opened in 1952, and it was a small chain at the time. Moss was the restaurant's manager when Coleman left to start his own chain called Tasty Bar-B-Q.

In 1962, William Loeb entered the field, and Coleman joined forces with him to create a chain called Loeb's Tasty Bar-B-Q. Loeb was the brother of former Memphis mayor Henry Loeb. The word *Tasty* was quickly dropped from the name as Moss was hired on during a period in mid-'60s, when he helped the chain open forty restaurants in thirty-six months. The location that became Three Little Pigs was opened by candlelight during a twenty-one-inch snowfall in 1965.

Richard McFalls photographs an old out-of-service pit off Chelsea Avenue in North Memphis for his "Memphis Barbecue Ghost Pit Chronicles" blog.

An example of a Memphis "ghost pit" on the side of a Quizno's sandwich shop on Highland near the University of Memphis. The building was once home to the Memphis area's final Little Pigs restaurant, which shouldn't be confused with Three Little Pigs. Little Pigs was a local chain founded in about 1950 by a man named Frank Howell. In 1962, a national chain called Little Pigs of America started after its owners contacted Howell to copy his business plan, according to Richard McFalls of the "Memphis Barbecue Ghost Pit Chronicles" blog. "It was all over the country, which is what made it different, but the performance never came close to the company hype," McFalls said. The Little Pigs of America filed for bankruptcy in 1967. The locally owned Highland location was still in business until well into the early 2000s.

A 1968 photo of a newly opened Loeb's Bar-B-Q at the northwest corner of Park and Loeb near the University of Memphis, where a Burger King sits today. *Courtesy of the Memphis and Shelby County Room, Memphis Public Library.*

An undated photo of a Loeb's Bar-B-Q at the corner of Summer and White Station, where the Gold Club strip club is located today. Memphis was notorious for the raunchy, anything-goes atmosphere of its strip clubs before several FBI raids in 2006 shut down multiple clubs and led to much stricter regulation of the remaining establishments. *Courtesy of the Memphis and Shelby County Room, Memphis Public Library.*

A June 6, 1965 article in the *Commercial Appeal* reported that "a joint venture by William Loeb and singer Pat Boone," whom Loeb had convinced to invest in the chain, wanted to average one new store per month. "We'd expand much more quickly, but our problem is getting trained personnel and supervisors to operate the outlets," Loeb said.

That statement ended up being prophetic. "It was too hard to find qualified help," Moss said. "We had store managers who could barely read and write. The problem with a barbecue shop like this," he said, nodding toward the Showboat dining room around him, "that's mostly a sandwich shop, there's not enough business volume to pay middle-management salaries. It kind of requires an owner on-site."

On July 3, 1965, the *Commercial Appeal* reported the opening of the twenty-fifth Loeb's Bar-B-Q store, a 1,600-square-foot space at 1669 Lamar that was the prototype for a new prefab layout. Six months later, on January 1, 1966, the *Memphis Press-Scimitar* reported that Loeb bought out the contracts of then-president and general manager Coleman; Coleman's wife, who was the secretary-treasurer; and Moss, who was the vice-president.

Coleman responded by starting his own chain, Coleman's Bar-B-Q, where Moss went to work while the feuding between Loeb and Coleman continued in the background. When asked why the partnership between the two men failed, Moss bluntly stated, "They were too busy trying to screw each other over." A search through newspaper records backs up that statement.

On April 7, 1972, the *Memphis Press-Scimitar* reported that A.B. Coleman received a two-year suspended sentence for two counts of tax evasion after Loeb reported him to the Internal Revenue Service (IRS). "It was brought out during the trial that Loeb had contacted an IRS agent and had supplied information which led to the indictments against Coleman."

During the trial, Loeb accused Coleman of using rebate checks from suppliers at Loeb's Bar-B-Q as personal income. Coleman claimed that he was forced to because Loeb was charging personal debts to the business, cutting into his share of the profits. Loeb's purchases through the business included $790 for dinners at Justine's restaurant and $1,090 for imported cigars, according to a January 4, 1972 article in the *Commercial Appeal*. At the time of the article, it was stated that Coleman owned ten Coleman's Bar-B-Q restaurants.

On February 6, 1974, the *Commercial Appeal* reported that Loeb's was ready to resume expansion. At the time, there were thirty Memphis locations and thirty-eight in other cities. All but five were franchises. A new franchise cost $30,000 for a complete package, with equipment, training, initial inventory and signs, first month's rent, first year's insurance and cash for change in the register. From there, Loeb got a 3 percent royalty on gross profits.

Instead of the expansion that Loeb had planned, the chain began to fall apart. Coleman's followed as expansion fatigue set in there as well, Moss said. Showboat Barbecue on Hickory Hill Road was a Coleman's "for about 20 minutes," he said. Moss bought and rebranded it and two other Coleman's sites as the chain was collapsing. He said that he dreamed up the name one night and trademarked it. Shortly after, he enjoyed a marketing advantage with the name during the short-lived lifespan of the United States Football League and its successful Memphis Showboats team, which operated for two seasons in 1984 and 1985. Despite having the name trademarked, Moss said, "I didn't do anything about it because everyone loved the Showboats, and I didn't want to be an asshole."

An advertisement for a Coleman's Bar-B-Q franchise location. *Courtesy of Richard McFalls.*

Moss is still at his remaining Showboat location every day and still cooks with the old Coleman's charcoal pit. "I'm one of the few people left in Memphis that still cook in a brick barbecue pit," he said. "You get all the smell and all the taste. It's becoming a lost art. It's hard, dirty, nasty; there's not many of us left that do it anymore." The brick pits don't have any timers or temperature gauges. Moss and his longtime employees, several of whom have been with him since the '80s, simply know what they are looking for in the fire and the meat. He cooks over natural hardwood lump charcoal lit with cardboard to avoid using chemicals.

Showboat Barbecue owner Porter Moss (*left*) with his sixty-year-old son, Jerrell Moss, who runs the restaurant with him.

Using a brick pit means paying attention to the weather outside. "If it's twenty degrees outside and you wait until 7:00 a.m. to fire the pit, you've got a bad day ahead of you." It isn't just a matter of getting the flame up to temperature. The bricks have to heat up before the meat can go in. Then there is the ever-pressing question of how much to cook. "It's not like hamburgers. You have to project because it takes some time to cook."

In another nod to the past, Showboat offers barbecue stew every year from October 15 through April 1. The recipe for the mix of pulled pork, corn, potatoes, tomatoes, onions, pinto beans and okra in a hearty broth came from a 1928 cookbook by then-famous food writer Henrietta Dull. Moss tweaked the seasonings and added the stew to his menu a decade ago. "I'm a Taurus. I can't dream up new stuff, but I can make old stuff better," he joked. During the cold-weather months, a bowl of the stew, served with corn bread muffins for sopping up the juice, is a satisfying, stick-to-your-ribs meal that Moss sells for less than seven dollars.

While the Loeb's and Coleman's chains faded away, the one that preceded them both is still thriving after more than sixty years of slow, steady growth. People commonly refer to Tops as "fast-food barbecue" because there are fifteen locations spread throughout the Memphis area where you can quickly grab cheap barbecue from either an inside counter or a drive-thru. But there is nothing fast about the cooking process. The company has steadfastly refused to adopt modern conveniences like gas-assisted pits or centralized off-site meat cooking. Every location cooks with charcoal and hickory in old-fashioned open pits. And unlike fast-food chains with a uniform, prefab design for their restaurants, each Tops has a unique layout and appearance.

When you're in Memphis, there is almost always a Tops nearby, so it sets the standard for "Memphis average" pulled pork. If you want to open your own barbecue place, you better be able to compete with them. Tops shoulder meat hits the right mixture of tender but meaty, and it has the flavor that makes charcoal pits worth the effort. So, the standard for barbecue from a Memphis drive-thru is better than anything many people in other parts of the country have tasted.

In a 2002 interview with Joe York for the Southern Foodways Alliance, Tops general manager George Montague said that the company strives to have a master cook at each location to maintain consistency:

> *It's not that complicated, but you've got to be vigilant. You're talking about eight or 10 hours of watching a pit, making sure that the pit stays even, making sure the fire doesn't go out, making sure it doesn't flare up too much…*
>
> *After they've cooked* [skin side down] *three quarters of the way done, then they turn the shoulder over on the meat side. When they turn it over on the meat side it does what we call "dripping out." It actually starts dripping out, the fat… At that time that's when there's the most danger for what we call a "pit fire." If that cook is not on the ball and watching what they're doing, they can burn up three or four hundred dollars worth of meat just like that *snaps his fingers*. But, of course, once they turn it over… and all the good cooks know how to do it…they continue cooking it until it drips out, gets completely done, and by turning it over that meat side takes on about a quarter-inch crispness—that's the outside meat, what you call brown barbecue.*

A big part of the secret to Tops' success is having a fairly limited menu. In the interview with York, Montague said that the chain generally cooks 1,200 to 1,500 shoulders per week. While Tops is still primarily a sandwich shop, it added ribs and brisket to the menu in recent years. The chain is also widely known throughout the Memphis area for offering one of the best double cheeseburgers around.

The burgers are a case study in simple perfection. The patties of fresh ground beef from Charlie's Meat Market on Summer Avenue are seasoned with salt and pepper before going on the grill. The buns are also toasted on the griddle; the cooked patties are added to one half, and the toppings are added to the other. This melds all the flavors together and soaks one of the bun halves with delicious grease before the whole glorious concoction is combined and secured into a wax paper sleeve with a toothpick holding it together. It isn't some big, fancy steakhouse burger. It isn't fast food either. Tops sells shoulder meat for forty-five cents per ounce, so for the ultimate Tops experience, order a burger topped with an ounce or two of pork.

While each location makes cole slaw fresh daily, both the dressing for the slaw and the barbecue sauces are made in bulk at the Tops headquarters/warehouse on Mount Moriah. Using the same well-balanced mustard and mayo dressing for the slaw at every location helps maintain the reliable Tops consistency. Another key to that consistency is the measured approach that the company has taken toward growth. While other chains grew at a frantic pace without regard to adequately training staff, Tops has expanded slowly enough to promote experienced managers and master cooks from within.

"The reason a lot of people haven't made it in barbecue, the reason they haven't been able to franchise a lot of these places out like we have, is because it takes so long to get that barbecue from that raw shoulder to that delicious sandwich. It takes so much care. It takes so much attention to detail," said Montague in speaking to the Southern Foodways Alliance.

Another group of investors attempted to expand Leonard's Pit Barbecue into a large chain. "They thought they could turn it into another McDonald's," said current owner Dan Brown. Brown began his career there during the era when Elvis Presley would visit the Bellevue store up the street from Graceland. "When I started in '62, he was still coming to the restaurant, but he was already so famous he only came when we were already closed," Brown said. Brown got the job through his uncle, a pastor at St. Paul's Catholic Church in Whitehaven where the Heubergers were members. Presley would call ahead to let the restaurant know that he would be coming by, and employees were forbidden from using the phone to tell others. As fans learned to hang out in the parking lot after hours anyway to look out for the famous singer, Presley had to start sending people from Graceland to pick up to-go orders instead.

Brown was a sophomore in high school when he went to work at the restaurant, staying there until he joined the army in 1967. Meanwhile, Leonard Heuberger sold the restaurant to an investment group headed by

Hoehn Chevrolet owner T.W. Hoehn, which was reported in the August 24, 1964 edition of the *Memphis Press-Scimitar*. After Brown returned to Memphis, he resumed working part time at Leonard's while attending Memphis State University on the GI Bill. He was the restaurant's general manager for nine years before he purchased it himself in 1993.

By then, the Leonard's Inc. investors had already closed most of the restaurants due to the same staffing challenges that hampered the Loeb's and Coleman's chains. Running a barbecue restaurant is enough of an ordeal that even one of Leonard's two grandchildren wanted nothing to do with it. "Being raised in it, I just wasn't that interested in it. There are two businesses you don't want to be in unless you want to work yourself to death, and that's a restaurant and a grocery store," said the seventy-six-year-old Bill Hughes. He retired from the *Commercial Appeal* newspaper, where he maintained mainframe computers, and now works as a beekeeper. His brother, Tommy Leonard Hughes, did embrace the family trade and owned the Tommy Leonard's Bar-B-Q restaurant in Horn Lake, Mississippi, for several decades before retiring in July 2011.

CHAPTER 4
DECLINE

The Loeb's and Coleman's chains dissolved during a low point for Memphis. In many ways, the trajectory of their rise and fall mirrored that of Stax Records. Founded as Satellite Records in 1957, the label changed its name to Stax in 1961 shortly after moving from the rural community of nearby Brunswick to its famed home on McLemore Avenue in South Memphis. When mentioning the soul music label in his book on the blues, Barlow wrote that "from 1963 to 1975 [Stax] went through one of the most spectacular boom-and-bust cycles in the history of the American music industry," bringing in more than $14 million annually during its zenith in the late '60s, when it was home to a roster including Otis Redding, Isaac Hayes, Rufus and Carla Thomas, Sam and Dave and Booker T. & the M.G.'s.

The early Stax singles included the 1964 song "Bar-B-Q" by Wendy René, an infectious ode to the city's signature food. The label suffered several major blows beginning when its biggest-selling star, Otis Redding, and all but two of the original members of the Bar-Kays were killed in a December 10, 1967 plane crash while headed to perform in Madison, Wisconsin. Shortly after, the sale of Stax distributor Atlantic Records resulted in Stax losing the rights to all its material released between 1960 and 1967. Then, on April 4, 1968, civil rights leader Dr. Martin Luther King Jr. was assassinated while standing on the balcony of the Lorraine Motel, a common hangout for Stax artists.

His murder was a devastating blow to race relations in the city and stifled the once-vibrant atmosphere at the famously integrated recording studio. "Stax Records was one of those anomalies that regardless of the segregation that existed in this town, and other areas of the time, it managed to put that aside and it was all about the music. If you could play, we didn't care," said Marvell Thomas, who compared it to "an oasis in the desert" during a March 2014 forum on the history of Stax at Rhodes College organized by Robert Gordon, the author of *Respect Yourself: Stax Records and the Soul Explosion.* Thomas, a gifted soul keyboardist whose session credits include Isaac Hayes's "Hot Buttered Soul," is the son of Rufus Thomas and brother of Carla Thomas. "The atmosphere changed a lot," he said of the period following the assassination. "People who had been friends for years suddenly began to mistrust each other. It was not a good place to be at the time."

King was in Memphis assisting striking sanitation workers. His killer, James Earl Ray, was an Illinois native who had become involved with the white power movement while living in Los Angeles. Ray had no ties to Memphis and only traveled to the city after failing to murder King in King's hometown of Atlanta, but Ray's act of terrorism forever tarnished the city's image.

Stax wasn't the only local institution damaged by the assassination. Henry Loeb was the mayor of Memphis during the sanitation strike, which resulted in him being labeled a racist by many black residents. In the book *Memphis Chronicles: Bits of History from the Best Times*, author John E. Harkins, who supervised the processing of Loeb's administrative files while working as the Memphis and Shelby County archivist in the early '80s, described Loeb as a man who unfairly earned a "bum rap" among scholars and the media.

The Loeb's Bar-B-Q chain owned by Henry's brother, William, became an instant target. Stores were vandalized and firebombed despite many of them being black-owned franchises, according to William's son, Bob Loeb. A column by Dan Conaway in the *Daily News* on April 30, 2010, described the longtime friendship between William Loeb and Howard Robertson, a black postal carrier and part-time waiter at the old Justine's restaurant who became a partner in several Loeb's Bar-B-Q restaurants earlier in the '60s. Despite the actual ownership of the restaurants, and the intentions of the Loeb family, the name represented authority in a time of rage against symbols of the establishment.

In another blow to the black community the same year as King's death, the urban renewal plan enacted by the Memphis Housing Authority removed about four hundred buildings from the mostly black neighborhood south of Beale Street, resulting in a period when there were more people in jail downtown than residents, according to Jimmy Ogle. The sixty-one-year-old Ogle is a lifelong Memphian who began managing the parks and recreation department in 1979. In 1985, he became the general manager for the newly opened Mud Island park and museum. In 1998, he went to work for John Elkington, helping with the redevelopment of Beale Street. In 2000, he became the director of the Rock and Soul Museum at the Gibson guitar factory, and he now serves as the general manager of Beale Street Landing, where tour boats dock at the western end of the historic street.

Stax declared bankruptcy on December 19, 1975. The city's music industry hadn't even begun to recover when Elvis Presley was found dead in his Graceland mansion a year and a half later on August 16, 1977. By 1979, there were about five hundred residents in the downtown area and one thousand inmates at the jail. "We built the only building in the city known just by its address at 201 Poplar," Ogle said of the jail. With the loss of their customer base, the retail businesses that had come to dominate Beale folded, with the exception of A. Schwab, a dry goods store founded in 1876 that is the only original Beale Street business left today. The street was fenced off from 2nd to 4th Street, and customers entered A. Schwab through an entrance along the back alley.

During the heyday of Stax, its musicians frequented restaurants around the studio like the Four Way, a famed soul food restaurant that is still open at the corner of Mississippi and Walker a few blocks from the Stax Museum at the old recording studio site. Another favorite was Culpepper's Chicken Shack, which closed in 1971 after a brutal robbery of owners Walter and Hattie Culpepper during which Hattie was pistol-whipped so severely that she remained hospitalized until her death in 1992, according to an account on Richard McFalls's "Memphis Barbecue Ghost Pit Chronicles" blog.

"Culpepper's was the best barbecue this town has ever had," said Marvell Thomas. "Brady and Lil's was second best. People are running around talking about the Rendezvous like that is the best barbecue. That's third- and fourth-tier stuff."

Brady and Lil's on South Parkway, which lives on today as the Bar-B-Q Shop on Madison in Midtown, was one of the city's first black-owned restaurants to gain a following of white customers. Legendary Memphis soul music producer Willie Mitchell took the Beatles there in 1964 while the band was visiting his Royal Recording Studio and rehearsing for its first U.S. tour. "'Man, we had a big party that day,' Mitchell remembers. 'They went around the corner to Brady and Lil's restaurant and bought up *all* the barbecue,'" according to the June 12, 2004 edition of the *Memphis Flyer*.

Brady Vincent was a former railroad cook who lived above the restaurant with his wife, Lil. Eric Vernon said that his family visited the restaurant every Friday. His father, Frank Vernon, was working as a UPS driver when Vincent mentioned that he was thinking about retiring. After Frank and his wife, Hazel, bought the restaurant in 1980, Vincent continued living above it for another year, mentoring the new owners.

Vincent trained the Vernons on how to operate the charcoal pit and taught them his recipes for making sauce, slaw and his signature barbecue spaghetti. From there, the Vernons developed recipes for dry rub, baked beans and the restaurant's rib glaze, as well as starting the tradition of offering Texas Toast in place of hamburger buns for pork sandwiches.

In 1983, the Vernons opened a second Brady and Lil's location at Knight Arnold and Mendenhall but quickly decided that they had spread too far. "We felt like we moved too far from our original crowd. We decided to look for somewhere in Midtown, where we would be between South Memphis and East Memphis," said Eric. The family consolidated its restaurant business at 1782 Madison in November 1987. Vincent had passed away, and the family planned to call the new restaurant Frank and Hazel's Bar-B-Q Shop when a friend suggested simply calling it the Bar-B-Q Shop.

The Vernons added a brick-and-steel charcoal pit inside the building that mimicked the one they'd cooked with in South Memphis. Years later, they added an additional gas-fired Southern Pride cooker in the back of the store to handle the steadily increasing volume of customers. Eric said that he burns hickory wood in the gas pit to maintain the smoke flavor customers have come to expect. While Jack's Rib Shack, the Three Little Pigs and the Bar-B-Q Shop all eventually incorporated the oft-maligned gas-fired pits into their kitchens, it is important to note that all three had owners with years of experience cooking with old-fashioned pits who carefully worked to re-create the flavor.

The gas-assisted pit was essential to cook enough high-volume foods like the Boston butts the restaurant uses for pork sandwiches. But the original charcoal pit isn't retired. "Nothing beats what you come from," Eric said. He uses it strategically for situations where he feels like the charcoal flavor is essential, like preparing the base for the restaurant's barbecue spaghetti. The family is famously tight-lipped about how the spaghetti is made, but Eric did say that one of the crucial steps involves smoking the base for at least twelve hours.

Barbecue spaghetti has been in Memphis for decades and shouldn't be confused with the barbecue and spaghetti half-and-half dinners that have an even longer history in the city. In the first half of the twentieth century, many of the biggest names in Memphis barbecue were Italian, according to Bill Hughes.

While his grandfather Leonard Heuberger was German, Leonard's wife, Edith (born Edith Sugliano), was Italian. Hughes said that she originated the tradition of offering the half-and-half plate of equal portions of pulled pork and traditional spaghetti at Leonard's. Barbecue spaghetti is an entirely separate dish created by Brady Vincent. It features barbecue meat and a delicious smoke-infused sauce in soft, overcooked spaghetti noodles.

Two Memphis restaurants with a direct connection to Vincent serve barbecue spaghetti today. When Vincent sold his restaurant to Frank Vernon in 1980, he taught Frank how to make the dish. And when Frank moved the restaurant to Midtown and changed the name to the Bar-B-Q Shop, he continued to offer barbecue spaghetti using the same recipe. It is still on the menu today. Meanwhile, Jim Neely grew up next to Vincent's mother and consulted Vincent when he was opening Interstate Bar-B-Q in 1979. Neely said that Vincent also taught him to make barbecue spaghetti, which he added to his menu in 1981.

While neither shared a full recipe, Neely said that his starts by taking the back flap of meat off a rack of ribs and putting it in a pot with bell peppers, onions, basil and parsley. Neely famously developed his own signature sauce, while the Bar-B-Q Shop still uses Vincent's recipe. So Interstate offers a take on the dish based on pointers from Vincent, while the Bar-B-Q Shop faithfully follows the original.

CHAPTER 5
MOVING EAST

Brady and Lil's eastward transformation into the Bar-B-Q Shop happened as the city's population was shifting the same direction. Barbecue followed, taking on a more polished image. As the Loeb's Bar-B-Q empire began its decline, one of its employees had a vision for a completely different approach. In 1975, Clyde Gridley opened a large restaurant on Summer Avenue just west of Graham from a Loeb's franchise, now Bryant's Breakfast, that he had owned.

Gridley was working as an accounting comptroller for Loeb's when "he saw the books for the Loeb's franchisees and said, 'Shoot, I'd rather do that,'" noted current Loeb's Property president Bob Loeb, who is the son of Loeb's founder, William Loeb. Bob worked for Gridley at his franchise store, making sandwiches for two years, starting as a sixteen-year-old in the summer of 1971.

Gridley's Bar-B-Q was unlike any restaurant Memphians had seen. Gridley hired waiters from the recently closed Peabody to tend tables in tuxedos with bow ties and wearing white gloves with towels draped over their arms. "That was *the* spot," Carl Johnson said of the restaurant, where Memphians waited hours for a table. Johnson began working at Gridley's as a teenager. He started out cleaning and worked his way up to busboy and then waiter and cook. He helped open the Macon location in 1979. Today, he owns Cave's Soul Food and More on Jackson Avenue with his wife, Veronica. The Cave's moniker is a combination of his and his wife's first names, and the restaurant has a charcoal pit for barbecue that he copied from the old Gridley's design.

On July 13, 1982, the *Commercial Appeal* reported Clyde Gridley's plans to start franchising his restaurant. A franchise would cost $100,000 plus 3 percent of gross profits at a time when a Wendy's franchise was $15,000 plus 8 percent, a Danver's was $10,000 plus 4 percent and a McDonald's was a staggering $275,000–$340,000 plus 11 percent. "One of our concerns is being able to get good ribs. It's not like a hamburger operation where you can get all kinds of suppliers," Gridley told the paper. "We even designed a special knife used to lift the ribs from the carcass to be sure more meat is left on the ribs."

Before he could carry out his franchise plans, Gridley died on what ended up being a monumentally tragic day for Memphis. On the morning of December 12, 1983, Gridley was killed when he had a heart attack while driving that caused him to wreck his car. Later that day, a plane crash claimed the lives of Memphis State University football coach Rex Dockery, assistant coach Chris Faros and star player Charles Greenhill, along with pilot, Glenn Jones, on their way to an awards banquet being held by the Lawrenceburg Quarterback Club in Lawrenceburg, Tennessee.

Gridley died months before the opening of a competitor that became one of the most recognized barbecue brands in the world. Donald Pelts came to barbecue from the furniture business when Donald's Furniture sold out in 1972. Looking for a new career, he purchased the Public Eye, a combination barbecue restaurant and bar in Overton Square during the Square's original '70s-era heyday. By '82, Pelts had become tired of the bar crowd and late weekend hours associated with it and began looking east to open a barbecue joint, according to his forty-six-year-old son, Barry Pelts.

His goal was to offer the kind of traditional charcoal- and hickory-cooked pork that was usually found in neighborhood barbecue joints but at a major crossroads between areas where people lived and worked. Many neighborhood restaurants did a good lunch business but slowed down later in the day. "There was great barbecue in the 'hood, but people wouldn't go there for dinner," Barry explained. Decades before the concept of "fast casual" became a restaurant industry buzzword, Donald had a vision of combining waiter service with a drive-thru.

He fixed his attention on a building at 5259 Poplar Avenue in East Memphis that is still home to the flagship Corky's. In 1984, it was the site of a failed barbecue restaurant. Donald wanted to make a go of it with the product and staff he had from the Public Eye, pessimistically explaining to family members, "When I fail, I'll know I went in with both guns loaded and did everything right," Barry said.

Public Eye pitmasters Robert Moye and Joe Lee Johnson joined Pelts at the new restaurant. Johnson still tends the flames for Corky's at its Germantown Road location, while Moye recently retired. The average manager at Corky's has been with the company for twenty-three years, while the average employee has been there for sixteen years, compared to a food industry average of nine months, Barry said. "The reason we're successful is the culture my dad built. You take care of people, and they'll take care of you."

Donald Pelts planned to call his new restaurant Porky's, but shortly before opening, he got a letter telling him that the name belonged to another restaurant forty miles outside Memphis. Undeterred, he simply changed the *P* to a *C*.

Like the Bar-B-Q Shop in Midtown and Leonard's Pit Barbecue on Fox Meadows, Corky's has adapted to success by incorporating gas-fired ovens, while keeping old-fashioned charcoal pits for ribs. It loads plenty of hickory wood into the gas ovens for real smoke. Corky's has always served St. Louis–cut spare ribs rather than baby backs. While the spare ribs are easier to mess up, Barry Pelts said that the superior flavor when they are cooked right makes them worth the extra care and attention. The restaurant uses shoulders instead of Boston butts since it pulls pork from them to order, and the layer of fat and skin protects the meat from drying out.

Frustrated by the increasing need to drive east to the suburbs for good barbecue, Jim Neely claimed and cleaned up a corner of the inner city to open Interstate Bar-B-Q in 1979, years before the rebirth of Beale Street to the north as a tourist district. "I am the Neely that put the Neely name in barbecue in Tennessee," he said with the fierce pride of a seventy-six-year-old entrepreneur who transformed a small grocery store on a rough corner into an internationally recognized brand. His passion for barbecue and obsessive attention to detail led to multiple expansions that created the current cavernous restaurant, which seats three hundred people and is where he still shows up every morning at 5:00 a.m.

A native Memphian, Neely joined the air force and moved to California after he graduated from high school in the '50s. When he left the service, he moved back to Memphis for a year in 1958 before returning to California, where he began a successful career as an insurance agent. He never forgot the Memphis barbecue from his childhood, though, and sought it out every time he returned home to visit. "When I came to Memphis, the first thing I wanted to do when I crossed that bridge was go to the 'hood and get some barbecue," he said. "I'd eat it every day I was here."

He returned for good in 1972, starting another successful insurance agency based in Memphis, with offices throughout the South. He was earning a six-figure salary (a huge sum in the '70s) with no intention of going into the barbecue business, when his oldest son, Kelvin, was discharged from the navy disabled.

"I was rolling. I bought this grocery in this riffraff corner to give him a job," Neely explained. "At the time I came here, it was probably one of the roughest corners anywhere in a major city in America." The grocery was flanked by a beer joint and a liquor store. "All the elements were here for hooliganism."

Neely saw the site's potential and didn't back away from the challenge of cleaning up the neighborhood along with the building. "If you're scared, you might as well be dead. We don't lay down. We stand up," he said. While he bought the grocery business in 1978, he bought the actual property in 1979, along with the surrounding businesses. When he shut down the bar, its former patrons attempted to keep hanging around outside, drinking, drugging and urinating on the building. Neely said he carried a .357 Magnum with him when he would step out and explain that "anything I own I control. I don't believe in calling the police. I call paramedics." His wife, Barbara, was just as determined. "She's the Warden," Jim Neely said. "Believe me, she don't get no shit off employees or customers. I've seen her throw men out with a billy club."

With the corner cleaned up and more property than they needed for just the grocery, Neely thought about the barbecue he loved from his youth. In the late '70s, Memphis barbecue was dominated by the fine dining approach of Gridley's. Neely enjoyed the food at Gridley's but missed the neighborhood joints he grew up visiting.

"My dream was to bring back that old flavor," Neely said. "Brady gave me a lot of pointers," he said of Brady and Lil's founder Brady Vincent. He also consulted a friend from his insurance days in California. James Compton was originally from Louisiana and owned a restaurant in Los Angeles called Jay Bee's Bar-B-Q, where Neely would eat ribs while he lived on the West Coast. With tips from Vincent and Compton, Neely designed his own custom-made pit. While it is fired with natural gas, it has a firebox where he burns a combination of charcoal and hickory.

Like his pit, Neely developed his barbecue sauce by combining his ingenuity with advice from others. "It took me about four years to develop that sauce. Older black people in the neighborhoods had sauce so good you didn't need meat; you'd just eat it on bread," he said. He consulted as many old-time barbecue cooks as he could, combining the best recipes. Meanwhile, his palate had expanded during his travels around the world with the air force, and he began to incorporate additional seasonings like paprika, chili powder and cumin. "Older black people didn't know anything about no herbs," he said.

Jim Neely inspects a slab of beef ribs at his Interstate Bar-B-Q restaurant on South 3rd Street. Neely was one of the first Memphis restaurant owners to offer barbecue beef products alongside the area's traditional pork-based fare.

Neely experimented with old and new recipes until he had his sauce perfected. "Now we ship it all over the country," he said. Today, he has a USDA-approved kitchen behind his restaurant that cooks six sixty-quart pots of sauce per day. It can also cook 1,700 pounds of meat at a time, which the restaurant overnight ships to anywhere in the United States.

Around the same time Neely was cleaning up his corner south of downtown, the Cozy Corner restaurant was building a following just east of the then newly opened Hernando de Soto Bridge carrying I-40 across the Mississippi River. While Interstate Bar-B-Q transformed from a small grocery offering barbecue into an enormous restaurant, Cozy Corner is still the same little neighborhood joint it was when it opened, despite a dramatic turnaround in the area around it, which was once dominated by the Hurt Village public housing projects.

If you want to truly feel like a caveman, try the primal experience of consuming a Cornish hen from the restaurant on North Parkway near Danny Thomas. It's a gloriously delicious mess. There is no way to look like a civilized human being while eating one. They are cooked in the same aging charcoal-only pit as the restaurant's outstanding ribs, sliced pork, chicken wings and bologna. No one knows the age or history of the old pit, which was already in the building when Raymond Robinson opened the Cozy Corner in August 1977, according to grandson Bobby Bradley, who mans the pit today.

Robinson passed away in 2001 at the age of sixty-five. Bradley doesn't know when the Cornish hens first appeared on the menu. "We've been doing it for a long time. I'm twenty-nine, and it's been here all my life," he said. The pit is a Chicago-style cooker with a glass-cased cooking chamber above a steel charcoal burn box.

During his three decades around the aging restaurant, Bradley has watched the area around it transform as the nearby St. Jude Children's Research Hospital has grown tremendously, while the sprawling housing projects that were just north of the St. Jude campus were demolished in 2000 for the Uptown community of mixed-income housing. It was the projects where National Football League star Michael Oher, whose story was told in *The Blind Side* book and film, originally lived.

"It used to be the freaking ghetto; Hurt Village. But at the same time, we had a lot of people who worked here who lived there. And a lot of kids from there would come here and order food. Some of them come back to visit and talk about my granddad. Some of them, he impacted their lives in a good way, whether it was a piece of advice or whatever. There's danger everywhere, but we've been blessed in this neighborhood," Bradley said. He motioned toward the direction of St. Jude and added, "They're doing such great things over there, [and] to have them close by, it's a good thing."

The Cozy Corner has one of the hottest hot barbecue sauces of any Memphis restaurant. At most barbecue joints, you'll find a sugary mild sauce and a "hot" sauce with a little bit of kick to it. The hot at Cozy Corner packs a deliciously fiery heat that builds steadily with each bite. "We actually make it hot," laughed Bradley. Workers at the restaurant have learned to warn first-timers about the level of spice. "A lot of people come in and say, 'Give it to me hot.' Then they complain that 'Whoa, this is hot!' We say, 'You asked for us to make it hot!' For the life of me I don't understand."

Luckily, the cole slaw at Cozy Corner is also good. Good slaw is vitally important when you crank up the spice on a barbecue sauce since it is where you turn for relief when your mouth starts to burn. It's like a Dirty South version of the yogurt-based raita that is an integral part of a satisfying Indian meal.

If you aren't sure if you can handle the heat, the restaurant has a medium sauce, although Bradley tries to avoid telling newcomers about it since he has had to replace so much food for people who don't seem to grasp that the medium will still have a noticeable kick to it. "The more choices you give people, the more mess-ups you have," he said. "Simple is better." The restaurant has a compact, well-crafted menu.

The pit requires constant attention, with someone keeping an eye on it the entire time the charcoal is burning. It has seen plenty of repairs over the years as heat has worn away metal and masonry. The heat also gives the ribs from the pit a charred exterior that can make them look burnt, but it is actually a delicious crusty bark surrounding a tender serving of smoky pork.

The meat is seasoned with a mix of standards like paprika, salt, pepper and chili powder. "When I finally learned how to make it, I was surprised by how basic it is," Bradley said. The secret is in the ratios. "You'll never get that out of me," he added.

Bradley wasn't sure if he wanted to work in the family restaurant when he went to college at Tennessee State University. He majored in business administration, looking for a degree that would give him as many options as possible. "You've got to be willing to sacrifice so much time. When it's all said and done, it's on your back," he said. Despite the long hours and hot work, he said, "When somebody takes a bite of something you cooked, and you look and you can see on their face they think it's great, it's such a satisfying feeling."

While the revitalization of the Uptown neighborhood and nearby downtown brought a lot of new customers, Bradley said that he wants the Cozy Corner to maintain the neighborhood restaurant atmosphere that it has developed alongside the building's timeworn patina. "I never want to get to the point that people say, 'Don't go there, it's too touristy.'"

That shouldn't be too much of a concern for Cozy Corner. It shares a timeless, unpolished atmosphere with beloved local sandwich shops like Payne's Bar-B-Q and the Morris Grocery, both of which occupy old, dimly lit buildings that appear nearly vacant. Payne's at least has a few tables and chairs spread out in the large, mostly empty dining area across from the little kitchen behind the order counter. Morris Grocery calls itself a grocery, but the large floor space in front of the order counter is completely empty other than a rack of potato chips, a small stand with some snack cakes and bread and a cooler for sodas and beer against the back wall.

While Morris started out as a country grocery, the Payne's building was originally a gas station. Its bricked-over service bay doors are still visible. Walk into either business, and there is a good chance you'll be the only customer there. Wait around and watch for a little while, and you will see a steady stream of customers dropping in to pick up a giant sandwich and leave.

Payne's is in the middle of the city on Lamar Avenue near McLean, while Morris is way out in the suburbs on Macon Road. Laddie Morris opened his grocery store forty-five years ago and started serving barbecue twenty years later. As the surrounding area transitioned from a rural community into a generic suburb, new businesses (like the large Kroger down the street) killed off his grocery business, so he shifted his entire focus to barbecue.

At Morris or Payne's, it is best to approach a jumbo sandwich with a fork. They are so overloaded with meat, sauce and slaw that the bun can disintegrate before you finish one unless you are wolfing it down. The Morris sandwich lets the meat be the star of the show. The pork is deliciously tender and packed with smoke flavor. The sauce is fairly sweet, but there isn't enough of it to overwhelm the taste. It balances well with the traditional mayonnaise-based slaw that features big enough chunks of cabbage to give the sandwich a nice crunch.

Meanwhile, a spicy Payne's sandwich is an exercise in battling extremes that combine to launch an all-out blitzkrieg on the taste buds. The intense sauce and slaw don't work when tasted separately. On a sandwich, the neon-yellow slaw combines with the red sauce and the meat to create a taste bud–jolting combination of vinegar, mustard, sugar, red pepper, tomato and charcoal smoke. The chopped pork has crunchy charred bark mixed in, providing an extra element of texture. Candice Payne-Parker said that the sauce and slaw were developed simultaneously by her grandmother Emily Payne, who founded the restaurant with Candice's parents, Horton and Flora Payne, in 1972, the year Candice was born.

The original Payne's location was at Lamar and Barksdale, but the family moved to its current location in 1976. Running the restaurant is still a family affair. When Horton Payne passed away in 1984 at the age of thirty-five, his wife, Flora, took over. Emily Payne passed away eight years ago at the age of seventy-two. A third generation of Paynes prepares her signature sandwiches today. The forty-one-year-old Candice and her thirty-five-year-old brother, Ronald Payne, grew up helping in the restaurant and are still in the kitchen with their mother every day, tending to the charcoal-only brick-and-steel pit.

The pit is fed by charcoal from another local institution that appeared around the same time as Payne's. The Charcoal Store on Florida Street has been supplying Memphis-area barbecue restaurants with cooking fuel since the mid-'70s. Owner Vernon "Pert" Whitehead said that he gets about fifty truckloads of charcoal per year, roughly one per week, with each truckload weighing in at forty-two thousand pounds. That works out to a little over one thousand tons per year, and that's just charcoal.

Whitehead also sells an assortment of woods like hickory, oak, pecan, apple and cherry. He said that roughly 85 percent of his sales are to area barbecue restaurants. The company has a delivery truck running four days a week that stops at about twelve to fourteen places each day. Area markets like Charlie's Meat Market and Easy Way produce stores make up most of the other 15 percent.

Individuals are welcome to shop there as long as they don't mind venturing into the section of South Memphis where the warehouse is located. If you want to hear an average Memphian react with complete terror, just call and tell them that you are lost in the city. When they ask where, say, "I'm somewhere south of downtown, and all the streets are named after states." It's an area known for poverty and crime, but it's also home to some outstanding examples of southern food. Deja Vu to the north on Florida has some of the best New Orleans Creole food in the city, while the South Memphis Grocery farther south on the same street has some of the best Delta-style hot tamales anywhere.

Despite the rough neighborhood, Whitehead said that the problems he's encountered have been fairly minimal. "I've never been threatened," he said. "I've had some trouble, but not as much as you'd think. I've had my AC unit stolen." When he first relocated to Florida Street in 1998, he made it a point to leave all his bay doors open during the day so anyone who wanted to case the place could see that all he had was big pallets of charcoal and wood. "They don't want to steal charcoal, and everyone knows that's all we got," Whitehead said.

The biggest time of year for dock sales to individuals is during the Memphis in May barbecue competition, when customers from around the world show up. If you need a single bag of charcoal, Whitehead will sell it to you. And if you show up with a flatbed truck needing several pallets, the staff will gladly load it for you with their forklift.

The business started when Whitehead's brother-in-law, Jim Schilling, was working at the old Royal Oak charcoal plant on Thomas in North Memphis, Whitehead said. When the company decided to close the plant, it offered Schilling three options: relocate to Atlanta, find another job or become a Royal Oak distributor in Memphis. Schilling and Whitehead opted to go into business for themselves, setting up in a warehouse around the corner from the old Royal Oak facility.

"We were hustlers out there hustling the business," the seventy-one-year-old Whitehead said. "I'm just coasting now." In 1981, the two men moved their operation to 136 G.E. Patterson in the South Main District, well before the current gentrification of that neighborhood. Today, that building is the

J&B Childress portrait studio, located in between the Double J Smokehouse and the downtown location of Central BBQ. The Charcoal Store moved on nearly fifteen years before the barbecue restaurants arrived.

While many competition teams insist on using natural lump charcoal, Whitehead said that briquettes have gotten a bad rap from cheap store brands. Cheap briquettes, like so many of the cheap products that line store shelves, are manufactured toward a price point regardless of what sacrifices in quality are necessary to reach that number. "They can make some and put so much garbage in there that if you burn it, no matter how long you let it burn down, it stinks like diesel exhaust."

Whitehead offers all-hardwood briquettes that are pressed from charred wood, with no added chemicals. Unsurprisingly, of the wood he offers, his bestseller is hickory, since the availability of hickory in the area made it one of the major smells and flavors associated with Memphis barbecue and one of the least expensive woods with which to cook. Among the fruitwoods offered at the Charcoal Store, apple is the biggest seller, followed by cherry.

In 1982, some restaurant owners were setting up in the suburbs offering the newly popular dry rub ribs with table service, while others were embracing the old neighborhood sandwich shop model. Jack Whitaker did both. He opened Jack's Bar-B-Q Rib Shack on Old Summer near White Station and bought a Loeb's Bar-B-Q location farther west on White Station at Quince that he rechristened Three Little Pigs.

"He also owned several dry cleaners around town. That's what he would do. He would buy a business and sell it after a couple years," said granddaughter Sharon Whitaker. When Jack sold the Rib Shack in 1983, the buyer was his son, Jack Whitaker Jr., who was largely talked into the purchase by Sharon's brother, Jack Whitaker III. Jack Jr. worked for the Illinois Central Railroad, and Sharon said, "I think dad got the restaurant mostly to keep us out of trouble."

It was during a different, more carefree era around Summer Avenue. While Sharon was a teenager, a cousin who helped run the restaurant would frequently lock her and her siblings in the restaurant after it closed at 1:00 a.m. so that her father could swing by and pick them up when his job at the railroad ended at 2:30 a.m. The building had a karaoke machine that the kids used to entertain themselves while they waited.

The Rib Shack served pulled pork, but its namesake food was offered either wet with sauce or dusted with a Rendezvous-inspired paprika and chili powder–based rub. Three Little Pigs was a pure sandwich shop. All the Loeb's locations had large metal signs in front of them of a cartoon pig holding up a Loeb's Bar-B-Q logo. Whitaker simply changed the top of the sign to represent the new name. It is the only Loeb's pig left in the city that hasn't been painted over.

Current owner Charlie Robertson bought the Three Little Pigs in 1989 and has been a constant presence there ever since. At the time he bought the restaurant, it was owned by a retired banker named Lynn Hobson. "He was one of those guys who thought you could just buy a business, stop in every week and collect your money. After six months, it was driving him crazy," said Robertson, who estimates that he puts in about sixty hours per week running the restaurant.

Robertson delivered bread for the Colonial bakery, and the Three Little Pigs was one of his stops. One day, Hobson asked if he was interested in owning a barbecue business. Robertson told him that he didn't have money for a down payment, and Hobson, who was eager to wash his hands of the enterprise, told him that this wouldn't stop him from making a deal.

Eating at the Three Little Pigs today is as close as anyone can get to the experience of visiting a Loeb's Bar-B-Q in the '60s. When Robertson bought the restaurant, one of the employees was Helen McClendon, who had been there since 1969, when she bought it as a Loeb's franchise before selling it in 1979 due to the long hours involved in running the establishment.

All the restaurant's recipes for sauce, slaw and beans came from McClendon, who passed away in 2011 at the age of eighty-five after working in the restaurant well into the 2000s. Robertson said that her expertise was crucial to his success in his early days as the restaurant's owner. "I haven't ever changed a one of our recipes. Barbecue is really subjective. What you like and think is great barbecue, I might not like," he said. "You've got to get that consistent quality." The Loeb's recipes handed down by McClendon, combined with her skill as a pitmaster, had already established a loyal customer base, so Robertson didn't tinker with a successful formula.

The subjective nature of barbecue also plays into Robertson's use of shoulders instead of Boston butts, due to the flavor he gets from all the additional fat, skin and bone. "We've done both. I think it's just a matter of personal preference. Some people won't touch shoulders, but I just prefer them," he said. Those shoulders are the main secret to the restaurant's thick, hearty baked beans, which start life as canned pork and beans. They get a generous serving of the bark from the shoulders added to them, along with some Three Little Pigs barbecue sauce, before they simmer. "That's where your best flavor is, so those beans pick up the smoke from that," he said.

CHAPTER 6

REVITALIZATION

John Elkington began working with the city to revitalize Beale Street during the early '80s, when the project was in desperate need of vision and leadership. He had to deal with the dual-edged sword of the street's history. "While many romanticized the musical history of Beale, the real Beale of the 1940s, '50s and '60s was pawnshops, crap games, bars and houses of prostitution," he wrote in his book on Beale.

Another huge problem was the condition of the buildings, which the city boarded up as it acquired them in the '70s. Sealing up the empty structures meant that they couldn't breathe during the boiling heat and humidity of Memphis summers, Elkington wrote. They filled with stagnant, steaming water that rotted away wood, plaster and masonry with shocking speed.

Beale Street was boarded up when the first Memphis in May barbecue contest was held just off Beale in a parking lot next to the Orpheum Theatre, which had also fallen on hard times. Built in 1928 for vaudeville performances, the Malco theater chain purchased it in 1940 and converted it to a movie theater. As the area around it declined, it began specializing in B-movies. When Malco decided to sell it in 1976, the final film shown there was a flick called *House of a 1,000 Pleasures*, according to Jimmy Ogle. In 1977, the Memphis Development Foundation purchased the building for $285,000, the same year that the annual month-long Memphis in May festival began with the goal of honoring a different country each year.

Organizers added the barbecue contest the following year in 1978. The first contest was a simple affair with twenty-six teams competing. Bessie

Louise Cathey from Mississippi won the $500 top prize cooking on a simple Weber grill. Despite its condition at the time, the Orpheum had already begun hosting concerts and Broadway musicals when the inaugural barbecue competition took place, but it closed for a period from 1982 to 1984 for a $5 million renovation.

Ogle was in charge of the city's parks and recreation department when the contest moved down the hill to Tom Lee Park next to the Mississippi River for its second year in 1979, when fifty teams entered. "Going from the asphalt lot to an eight-acre park with the river view was a big turning point that gave it a much more festive atmosphere," Ogle said.

One of the teams competing that second year was dubbed the Memphis Midtown Master Basters. While the team later cleaned up the name to the Crosstown Neighborhood Association, reflecting the Crosstown neighborhood in Midtown, it has competed at Memphis in May ever since.

Crosstown member Bob Reisling has been attending since that second year, when organizers decided to hold the event under a giant circus tent without considering the amount of smoke generated by fifty cooking teams. "They damn near killed everybody," Reisling said. He recalled teammate Dr. Paul Thompson pulling contestants out of the tent and reviving them as they hit the ground from smoke inhalation.

In those days, the contest was a far cry from the huge, highly organized event it is today. "There were no fences. It was nothing like today with the big tents and everything," said Reisling, a seventy-two-year-old professor emeritus with the Memphis College of Art. There were no portable toilets. People just used the riverbank. "Those early years were pretty rough. It was a big party, but you had to be really aware." Teams that left their areas unattended at night frequently returned to find all their food gone.

Reisling's team designated one team member to stay awake each night, armed and completely sober. "I remember one night when it was my turn, I held the pistol to the back of a kid's head. He had the cooker open and was about to shovel all our meat into a cooler." In those early days, teams cooked three shoulders—one for each of the two judges who would visit and one to set back in case they made it to the finals. The rules stated that after each judge visited, the rest of the shoulder had to be served to spectators. Chaos would follow, with mobs swarming for free barbecue. "I think that was when people began to realize they needed to make it more organized," Reisling said.

By 1981, the contest was drawing 180 teams from nine states and was patrolled by the police. "It's for the best," Reisling said of the steadily increased security. "An event that big could get out of hand real fast." The

'80s also brought fences and ticketed entry. "By then, the corporations were putting up the big outfits and the big rigs. That was also around the time the circuit got going. When they started, there was no such thing as sanctioned judges. It was whoever you could get." He recalled being judged by a girl visiting from California who said, "I've never had barbecue. I hope I like it." The circuit Reisling referred to was a series of Memphis in May–sanctioned contests throughout the country featuring certified judges.

Reisling's first taste of barbecue came just a few years before his first time cooking at Memphis in May. A self-described "ex-Yankee, born-again Southerner," he was born and raised in Iowa and taught school in Minnesota before abandoning the cold winters to find a job in the South, ending up at the Memphis College of Art. "We were out walking one day and came across a Tops Bar-B-Q. After we ate it, I told my wife, 'We've got to figure out how to cook this.'"

He bought a used fifty-five-gallon barrel cooker and attempted cooking a shoulder "like it was a steak or something. The whole thing was six-feet high in flames." A neighbor who saw the flames advised him about indirect heat and told him about coating the meat with mustard and seasoning with salt and pepper before cooking. "So I tried it and damn it came out pretty good." As an entry-level college instructor, Reisling was bartending part time at Zinnie's on Madison for extra money and worked mescal into his marinade.

"I didn't get anything out of any cookbooks. I just played," he said. "When I did the cooking, I just played by the seat of my pants." The team placed as high as second place in shoulder. Graduation for Memphis College of Art always seemed to fall the same Saturday as judging and usually ended around 11:30 a.m., while cooks had to be present for the judges at noon. A sunburned Reisling would attend graduation and have his son parked out front waiting with a change of clothes to rush him downtown.

Memphian John Willingham was a pioneer in combining success with Memphis in May and the restaurant industry. A sharp-minded inventor, entrepreneur and politician, Willingham designed and patented the pellet-fed rotisserie cookers he used in competitions and his restaurants.

His W'ham Turbo Cooker was an elaborate contraption that other teams laughed at the first time he showed up at Memphis in May with it in 1983. The laughter stopped when he won first place in ribs and the grand championship that year. He backed it up with another grand championship and first place in ribs in 1984. He also won the grand championship at the American Royal Invitational in Kansas City, Missouri, in 1991, as well as the grand championship reserve along with "Best Sauce on the Planet" there

One of the original W'Ham Turbo Cookers invented and patented by John Willingham, who used the creation to win back-to-back Memphis in May grand championships in 1983 and 1984. The cooker now belongs to Clay and Karla Templeton. Karla is one of Willingham's three daughters.

in 1992, giving him and his cooker the rare distinction of back-to-back top success in both Memphis and Kansas City barbecue.

Area cook Brent McAfee worked in Willingham's restaurant on Brookhaven Circle before it burned down in the mid-'90s. "Before we rubbed the shoulder, brisket and ribs down, we marinated it with a mix of apple cider vinegar and orange juice to open up the pores in the meat to allow the rub in," McAfee said. Willingham stressed the importance of having enough salt in dry rub to pull moisture from the meat to mix with the rub and create a marinade. His rub recipe, detailed in his book *John Willingham's World Champion Bar-B-Q*, is heavy on salt and brown sugar as opposed to the Rendezvous-inspired paprika-based rubs traditionally common in Memphis. The rub is still commercially made and available in stores and online.

Once the meat had been coated with rub, it marinated for twenty-four hours before going on the cooker, where Willingham carefully aimed for just the right amount of flame to get a steady 225-degree temperature with just enough smoke. Willingham identified the first three hours of cooking as the most crucial to flavor. After that, the bark on the surface of the meat seals it against absorbing more smoke.

Willingham looked for enough heat to avoid simple smoking, which occurs at temperatures under 225, while avoiding the grilling that occurs above 250 degrees, McAfee said. Barbecue is technically cooked not smoked, which implies curing at lower temperatures. But slow cooking with indirect heat

The burned-down original location of William's Bar-B-Q in West Memphis.

William's Bar-B-Q owner William Maxwell sitting in the current location.

Brady and Lil's on South Parkway as it looked in the 1960s. *Courtesy of Richard McFalls.*

Eric Vernon stands in front of the old charcoal pit at the Bar-B-Q Shop on Madison Avenue.

A Coletta's barbecue pizza.

Pitmaster Damon Briggs working in the smokehouse behind the South Memphis A&R Bar-B-Q.

Price board at the Charcoal Store on Florida Street.

Employee Curtis Simpson Jr. at the Charcoal Store on Florida Street.

Barbecue sandwich from Coleman's Bar-B-Q in Hernando, Mississippi.

One of the last remaining Coleman's Bar-B-Q locations in Hernando, Mississippi.

Bobby Bradley mans the same pit at the Cozy Corner that his grandfather Raymond Robinson used when the restaurant opened in 1977.

The Cozy Corner on North Parkway.

Ronald Payne at Payne's Bar-B-Q. *Courtesy of Rob Bellinger, manicamerican.com.*

Helen Turner making a shoulder sandwich at Helen's Bar-B-Q in Brownsville, Tennessee.

Ribs coming out of the smokehouse at Latham's Meat Company in Jackson, Tennessee.

Jack's Bar-B-Q Rib Shack on Old Summer before it closed.

Sharon Whitaker at Jack's Bar-B-Q Rib Shack before she closed the doors at the restaurant founded by her grandfather Jack Whitaker. *Courtesy of Dan Meade, manicamerican.com.*

Lump charcoal burns in the old-fashioned brick pit at Showboat Barbecue on Hickory Hill Road.

The Porky Pilots, a competition team of FedEx pilots, enjoys the festivities at the Memphis in May barbecue competition in the early '80s. *From left*: Bill Rochette, Steve Kuhar and Moke O'Connor. The team was formed in 1983 and took home a first-place victory in the whole hog category, according to team member and retired pilot Tom Webb. "I think the pilot's hat on the pig head was my idea," Webb said. *Courtesy of the Memphis and Shelby County Room, Memphis Public Library.*

A vat of coleslaw being prepared at Central BBQ on Central. Co-owner Craig Blondis said that it is enough to last the restaurant "several hours."

Ruth Gaines assembles sandwiches on the hot griddle at Leonard's.

This page and next: Tops is a chain, but every location has its own identity. Shown here are the Tops Bar-B-Q locations on Rhodes at Getwell, on Lamar and on Thomas in Frayser, as well as workers wrapping up construction on the newest Tops location on Poplar.

A Tops double cheeseburger with everything, topped with two ounces of pulled pork and barbecue sauce.

Mark Lambert of two-time Memphis in May grand champion team Sweet Swine O' Mine tends to shoulders during a competition.

Richard Lackie (left) and Blake Marcum of two-time Memphis in May grand champion team Sweet Swine O' Mine rush to prepare ribs for judges during a 2014 Memphis Barbecue Network invitational competition at Tiger Lane in front of the Liberty Bowl Memorial Stadium in Memphis. Tiger Lane was also the site of the 2011 Memphis in May barbecue competition when the Mississippi River flooded and forced the competition to move from its traditional home at Tom Lee Park next to the river..

Tucker Cookers under construction at the plant in downtown Memphis.

Top: Rib tip fried rice from KC's Southern Style Rice on South 3rd.

Middle: Richard Forrest cooks barbecue outside the Hi-Tone on Cleveland.

Bottom: Beale Street in its modern, revitalized state.

allows the meat to absorb a heavy smoke essence. Willingham tested barbecue with a fork to see when it was done, looking for a level of tenderness that would allow him to turn the fork with no resistance, McAfee said.

In his book, Willingham identified the five key elements to prize-wining barbecue as appearance, aroma, taste, texture and memory. When it comes to sauce, he wrote, "I am convinced sauce was invented to cover up mistakes in cooking." He was still a fan of the extra flavor that came from a dash of good sauce, writing that "thirty years ago, Memphis was strictly a vinegar-pepper sauce town, but about twenty years ago we witnessed the addition of tomato and brown sugar to some sauces. It crept in slowly but surely, and we have adopted such sauces with gusto—although our tomato-based sauces are more vinegary than others. We like some bite!"

As the barbecue contest was growing in popularity, Elkington was busy overseeing the redevelopment of Beale Street. While it reopened to the public in 1983, none of the initial wave of new restaurants was successful. Preston Lamm was a real estate consultant for Elkington at the time, and the two decided that the only way to make the street a success was to seed it with venues offering Memphis-specific music and food, foisting Lamm into the business. The 1985 opening of the Rum Boogie Café in a former tailor shop at 3rd and Beale signaled a turning point in the street's revitalization; 3rd Street is the name for the legendary "Blues Highway," Highway 61, which follows the Mississippi River from Minnesota all the way to New Orleans, Louisiana, as it passes through Memphis. So, the corner of 3rd and Beale represents the intersection of two of the most important roads in the history of American music.

"I grew up in Memphis, and I knew a lot of musicians who had moved out of Memphis due to lack of work," said Lamm, who is still president of Rum Boogie Café. Elkington and Lamm found blues musician Donn McMinn playing in a hotel in Little Rock, Arkansas, and hired him to put together a house band to play every night at the Rum Boogie. The club accumulated an impressive collection of Memphis music memorabilia, including the original Stax letters from the label's marquee that Lamm rescued when the original Stax building was demolished in 1989. "We got them out of the dumpster," Lamm said. "We had no money to buy anything." Instead, the club advertised with coupons that allowed patrons to exchange music memorabilia for free food and drinks.

The Rum Boogie Café also helped bring barbecue to Beale. The club started with a small kitchen serving New Orleans–inspired fare. But visitors constantly asked about Memphis barbecue, so Lamm got a small barbecue

The boarded-up future home of the Rum Boogie Café at 3rd and Beale. *Courtesy of the Memphis and Shelby County Room, Memphis Public Library.*

cooker from Walmart and set it up on the back patio. Before long, he had to buy a bigger one, and by the early '90s, the number of barbecue cookers on the patio had reached a point where Lamm had the restaurant's current electric Ole Hickory pit installed.

Unfortunately, since the buildings on Beale Street weren't designed as barbecue restaurants, they didn't have built-in traditional brick-and-steel pits. "Beale was just a commercial street like Poplar Avenue," Jimmy Ogle said. "It had hardware stores, grocery stores, lawyers' offices, wig stores, clothing stores." On a street with no traditional barbecue infrastructure, and where most people dining are tourists, boiled ribs and gas- and electric oven–cooked approximations of barbecue are sadly common. For people who work up a hunger barhopping on Beale, there is nothing wrong with grabbing an order of ribs there. But overly sweet sauces and rubs, a lack of smoke and claims of competition success that don't match with the food served seem to be the unifying features of most Beale Street barbecue.

The atmosphere of somewhere like the Silky O' Sullivan's or Alfred's patios or the live music somewhere like B.B. King's Blues Club or Rum Boogie make Beale Street an integral part of the Memphis experience, and all of them offer serviceable ribs. But people who ask where to go on Beale to try some of the city's best barbecue don't realize the oxymoron they are loading into their question. While talking about the modern spread of gas and electric cookers with Pert Whitehead at the Charcoal Store on Florida, it seemed natural to question him about the section of Memphis where clouds of smoke are so conspicuously absent. "We don't have any customers on Beale Street these days," he said.

Still, it is hard to exaggerate how far-fetched Elkington's dream of reinventing Beale as a successful entertainment district where black and white residents and tourists enjoyed themselves together seemed in the early '80s. Today, it is the largest-grossing tourist attraction in the state of Tennessee.

A few blocks from Beale, the Rendezvous still occupies the alley location across from the Peabody to which it moved in 1968. The alley is now flanked by a Holiday Inn and a Benchmark Hotel, while the restaurant's sausage and cheese plates and barbecue nachos are also served a block north at the Autozone Park Minor League Baseball stadium. Within a few decades, downtown has transformed from a blighted area to a thriving mix of commercial and residential redevelopment.

The popularity of barbecue nachos at the ballpark turned them into a regional specialty. They are so popular that they have begun to rival barbecue sandwiches in sales at many restaurants. They first appeared on a restaurant menu at the Germantown Commissary in 1982, one year after the restaurant opened in what had been a ramshackle country store dating back to the late 1800s next to the train tracks in old Germantown. Owner Walker Taylor frequently does concessions at horse shows in Germantown, and one day, he noticed employee Rosie Mabon piling barbecue on nachos she was making for herself. "I asked what they were, and she said, 'What do you think they is, fool? They barbecue nachos.'"

After sampling them, Taylor added them to the menu. They were an instant success. The concept is simple: a bed of chips covered with barbecue, cheese and barbecue sauce. Extra toppings like jalapeños, tomatoes and onions can add additional flavor.

Taylor's father owned the Commissary building during the end of its time as a country store. Along with standard general store wares, he sold food like barbecue, sliced bologna and deviled eggs. It was a common lunch stop for construction workers when Germantown was transitioning from a rural town into the affluent suburb it is today. As the construction work slowed down, Taylor, sick of working in the corporate world, converted it into a sit-down restaurant in 1981. Every barbecue plate sold there still includes one of the little deviled eggs made with the same recipe from the building's days as a country store.

Taylor uses old-fashioned charcoal pits for tasks like simmering beans, but he has transitioned most of the barbecue cooking to gas-fired Southern

Pride pits loaded with charcoal and hickory to handle the volume of food the popular restaurant handles and to avoid the risk of a pit fire. He is still haunted by the memory of a pit fire he suffered during his early days with the business. When asked when the fire occurred and how long he was closed for repairs, he didn't hesitate before answering, "September 13, 1984, at 9:23 a.m. I'll never forget. We were closed for ninety-one days." He added that "insurance companies are almost dictating a switch to the gas pits" due to the risk created by the old charcoal ones.

While barbecue nachos were a success for the Commissary, they didn't take the entire Memphis area by storm until 1998, when the Memphis Redbirds minor-league baseball team moved to Memphis and Ernie Mellor at Hog Wild Catering got the concessions contract to sell barbecue at Tim McCarver Stadium, where the Redbirds played before the construction of Autozone Park downtown. Mellor had been catering since the early '80s but had just gone full time with it the year before.

The team's food and beverage director, Jason McAulley, asked Mellor during an interview if he could be creative. Mellor, a friend of Taylor's, told him about barbecue nachos and said, "You watch; we'll have a line out the door." Once again, the dish was an instant success, this time with crowds from all over the city. "Everybody and their brother saw that we had a hot potato and started copying it," Mellor said.

Mellor's Hog Wild competition team has placed second at Memphis in May three times. An avid outdoorsman, the fifty-year-old said that he started cooking at deer camp in high school. From there, he initially took up competition barbecue because "it seemed like a good excuse to drink a beer." Today, along with Hog Wild, he also owns an upscale catering company called A Movable Feast. When he caters nachos today, he serves them on chips he makes by frying and seasoning cut-up flour tortillas instead of traditional corn chips.

Barbecue nachos have become so popular that it is hard to find a Memphis barbecue restaurant that doesn't serve them. The dish is a foolproof crowd-pleaser. People frequently praise restaurants by saying "the barbecue nachos there are incredible." The reality is that if a barbecue joint manages to turn out bad barbecue nachos, you probably don't want to try anything else from the kitchen.

CHAPTER 7
SMOKEHOUSE

While Memphis witnessed periods of tremendous change, there is a world of rural west Tennessee barbecue in which the appearance of the cars in the parking lots is the only indicator of the passage of time. At fifty-eight years old, Helen Turner has owned and operated Helen's Bar-B-Q in Brownsville, Tennessee, for eighteen years. She doesn't use any dry rub for seasoning the shoulders she cooks. She doesn't buy charcoal. She makes her own coals out of hickory and oak. Her barbecue pit is a crude homemade sheet metal and cinder block box sitting in the back corner of the screened-in porch behind her restaurant.

Turner actually has three pits. There is the warming pit inside the restaurant for shoulders she is pulling meat from for customers. There is a pit for cooking. And then across the screened patio from the cooking pit is the fire pit. Every morning, her husband stops in and builds a fire on his way to the Haywood Company belt and hose plant, where he has worked for thirty-six years. Turner said that she goes through two dump truck loads of wood per week. She feeds her cooking pit entirely with coals created by the logs burning down in the fire pit, transferring them herself one shovel-full at a time.

When questioned about her seasoning technique for her shoulders, she said, "I don't put anything on it—just that flame back there." Turner's style of cooking is deceptively simple. "I know what the coals got to look like and what the meat feels like when it's done," she said. The results are outstanding. Everything in the kitchen is made from scratch. Along with shoulder meat, she sells ribs and barbecue bologna. The sides she offers

Fire burning to feed the pit at Helen's Bar-B-Q in Brownsville, Tennessee.

are baked beans, potato salad and cole slaw, all made using old stoves, food processors and Crock-Pots scattered throughout the restaurant's aging kitchen. She goes through a few food processors a year chopping the roughly ten heads of cabbage a day she uses making slaw. The slaw has a perfect balance of mustard and vinegar. The meaty baked beans are served straight from a simmering Crock-Pot. And the potato salad is absolutely divine—light, creamy and packing just enough mustard.

The dining area at Helen's is a small space with two large tables surrounded by chairs. Black and white, young and old, the customers sit together to enjoy their food. There is usually a line of people waiting to order, but the friendly crew in the kitchen keeps it moving, led by Turner wielding her meat cleaver. The most common order is a chopped pork sandwich, topped with slaw and either hot or mild sauce. When a customer asks for a sandwich at the little order window separating the dining area from the kitchen, Turner turns around and pulls a fresh handful of smoked meat from one of the shoulders in the warming pit, chops it and assembles the sandwich with the speed and precision that come from decades of practice.

Even though tucked away in a small town of just over ten thousand people fifty miles from Memphis, barbecue as good as Turner's doesn't stay a secret. She's been featured in both *Garden & Gun* and *Southern Living* magazines, and in 2012, the Southern Foodways Alliance awarded her its Ruth Fertel Keeper of the Flame Award. While most of her customers are local regulars she knows by name, the national recognition she has garnered brings a steady flow of out-of-town visitors making the short trek to her restaurant from the stretch of I-40 between Memphis and Nashville.

Barbecue is an art where race and gender are irrelevant to the final product. The proof of the pitmaster is on the plate. Turner is a black woman. And Paul Latham is a white man who owns and operates Latham's Meat Company farther west of Brownsville in Jackson, Tennessee. With a population of just over sixty-five thousand, Jackson is big enough to support a number of barbecue restaurants but small enough for them to be serving rural-style west Tennessee barbecue to local repeat customers. There aren't any tourist traps to be wary of. Per capita it has to have one of the greatest concentrations of great barbecue restaurants in the world.

You can find dependably excellent ribs at Reggi's Bar-B-Q in front of the Pringles Park Minor League Baseball stadium, at Brooksie's Barn just off the 45 Bypass on Oil Well Road and at Back Yard Bar-Be-Cue across the street from the Old Hickory Mall. But even in that field of talent, there is something special about Latham's Meat Company. It sits along Highway 45 on the north end of Jackson, where the city begins to transition to fields, and the locals definitely know about it. On any given day, the breakfast-and lunch-only restaurant's large parking lot is packed with cars. But it isn't a place that gets mentioned in the press. Even in nearby Memphis, most people haven't heard of it.

Latham's is a combination old-fashioned butcher shop, barbecue restaurant and deer processor. There is nothing fancy about the place. Once you go through the front door, you are in an aisle that takes you past a row of drink coolers and freezers full of produce along one wall and then past the large butcher section occupying the back of the store before you finally reach the cafeteria-style area for ordering prepared food.

The food comes on a Styrofoam plate on a plastic tray with plastic utensils. Once you've made your selections and paid at the register, the dining area matches the cafeteria setting of the order counter. But the ribs are charred crispy on the outer edges, tender and juicy in the center, deeply pink to the bone and pack a complex smoke flavor. They aren't dusted with rub. They come naked and delicious. They are the type of simple, honest ribs that would score terribly at a barbecue competition, where the goal is a bite or two of flavor overload. It's a taste to be savored as a meal. The slaw, which looks like a damp pile of shredded cabbage and carrot with no mustard or mayo, has a surprisingly complex taste, with a good vinegar kick balanced with sweet and spicy elements.

Latham's has a large cinder block smokehouse behind it surrounded by big piles of wood and several fifty-five-gallon barrels in which hickory wood is burned down to create lump coals. "It is a lot more expensive to do it that way," Latham said. He buys his wood from a middle Tennessee sawmill that makes hickory panels. He has been in the meat business for fifty years, with twenty-five years in Lexington, Tennessee, followed by twenty-five years at his current location. "I could put electric or gas cookers out there and do it a lot cheaper, but I believe in doing it the original way," he said.

That original way includes a twenty-four-hour cook time for shoulders. "No fat, no waste, no taste," Latham said of the leaner Boston butts he shuns. The shoulders require constant vigilance during the first fourteen hours of the cook. By the final ten hours they are wrapped in foil and left largely unattended. "They finish themselves," he said. "If it wasn't for wrapping them in foil, you couldn't leave them." Latham said that a small pit fire can be extinguished by "popping it with a shovel." He uses vinegar to extinguish bigger flare-ups. "Three to six hours in is the danger zone," he said. Although a detached smokehouse removes the risk of a fire destroying the restaurant, pit fires are still a constant concern since no restaurant owner wants to see a valuable load of meat suddenly incinerated while customers wait inside.

One of the biggest keys to avoiding fires is keeping the pits clean, Latham said. Every week, the grates are scrubbed clean, and the ash pit beneath is completely cleared out. "If you don't do that, you get big plots of grease in it; then if you have a pit fire you're in trouble," he said. The pits are kept around 250 degrees with no thermometer. "I can tell by my hand." The smokehouse is full of individual pits, both inside it and along its porch-covered western wall. On July 4, Latham said that he typically cooks about one thousand shoulders, and for Thanksgiving, he sells one thousand smoked turkeys. The turkeys are available year round but require a day's notice.

The fire is usually manned by Mark Dalton, who has been with Latham's for seven years. "If you ain't doing this, it ain't barbecue," he said while moving a shovel-full of coals from one of the fifty-five-gallon burn drums to one of the pits inside the smokehouse. "That's why [the customers] keep coming back." Each barrel has an access hole big enough for a shovel cut into the bottom of it that Dalton uses to scoop out coals that have burned down from the wood added into the top. Occasionally, he picks out a whole flaming log and adds it to the pit, but he mostly cooks over an even bed of red coals. He relies on a gut instinct honed by experience. "It's a lot of work. You gotta enjoy what you do," he said as he fed coals to another pit. Ribs only cook for around three hours and are never wrapped in foil.

The reasoning behind a detached smokehouse is simple. Old-fashioned charcoal pits allow drippings from the meat to land on the burning embers

Pitmaster Mark Dalton sorts through the piles of wood outside the smokehouse at Latham's Meat Company in Jackson, Tennessee. Dalton burns down the wood in the surrounding barrels to create coals for the restaurant's pits.

below and flame up to impart an unmatchable flavor, but it comes with constant risk. Isolate the pits into a separate brick-and-steel structure, and you don't have to worry about a fire burning down the restaurant. Detached smokehouses are common behind barbecue joints in rural areas where space and close neighbors aren't an issue. But there is one restaurant inside the city of Memphis cooking the type of smokehouse barbecue that usually requires a road trip to the country to experience.

The A&R Bar-B-Q on Elvis Presley Boulevard in South Memphis opened in a small building with an indoor pit in 1983. The site of the original building is now a parking lot next to the current restaurant, according to pitmaster Damon Briggs. The forty-five-year-old Briggs began working at A&R shortly after it opened while he was a fifteen-year-old attending nearby Hamilton High School. After about fifteen years, the restaurant had outgrown the old location and moved to its current home. The little pit was relocated to the new location's kitchen, but it had a tendency to fill the place with smoke. After a year of fighting with it, A&R founder Andrew Pollard built the smokehouse behind the restaurant to house the little old pit along with two bigger ones.

A well-seasoned pit has bricks and steel saturated with smoke and grease that add an extra depth of flavor to anything cooked in them. The smokehouse behind the South Memphis A&R is infused with barbecue essence. It's a simple brick room with three charcoal-fired pits lining its south wall. Like Helen Turner at Helen's, Briggs earned most of the responsibility for watching the pits by simple fact of being one of the few people who can tolerate the smoke. Despite the heat, smoke and soot, he said that he enjoys the job, and he has developed an experienced eye for meat and coals.

The A&R name came from the first initials of founder Andrew Pollard and his wife, Rose. Andrew's father, Alonzo Pollard Jr., was a skilled backyard barbecue cook who passed down a passion for the craft. A slogan on the restaurant's wall reads, "Anyone can put the heat 2 the meat but only a few can Bar-B-Q." Andrew's daughter, Lashun Pollard Tate, runs the Hickory Hill A&R location, which opened in 2001. Andrew's brother, Alonzo Pollard III, is the father of Tarrance Pollard, who owns Pollard's Bar-B-Q just south of Graceland on Elvis Presley Boulevard. Alonzo III makes the homemade hot link sausages sold at A&R and Pollard's. Today, there are grandchildren and great-grandchildren of Alonzo Pollard Jr. working in the family's barbecue joints throughout the city. In another nod to the past, the fried pies at A&R are prepared using the recipes of a longtime cook from the still-remembered Justine's restaurant, which was once a Memphis fine dining landmark, who went to work at A&R after Justine's closed.

All the restaurants owned by Pollard family members cook with charcoal pits, but only the South Memphis A&R has a detached smokehouse, which had to be rebuilt following a bad pit fire in early 2014 that occurred while Briggs was on vacation and an inexperienced co-worker tried his hand at cooking. The main restaurant building was unscathed, reinforcing the value of a detached pit building. Briggs used outdoor barrel cookers until workers finished rebuilding the smokehouse around the old steel pits. The flavor from the smokehouse beats all the other A&R locations, especially when it comes to ribs. The ribs from it are tender yet meaty and pink all the way down to the bone. The smokehouse is the only seasoning necessary for the pork. "We cook fresh," said Brian Pollard, the forty-one-year-old son of Andrew Pollard who helps run his father's flagship restaurant. "No seasoning, straight on, pure smoke."

The ribs can be served dusted with dry rub or covered with sauce but are good enough to eat plain with just a small container of the restaurant's sauce to dip the occasional bite in. "That draws the customers," said Brian Pollard, motioning toward the smoke billowing from the smokehouse's three chimneys.

CHAPTER 8
SOLE SURVIVORS

The South Memphis A&R Bar-B-Q is just a mile and a half down the road from where the famed Bellevue and McLemore location of Leonard's was. Elvis Presley Boulevard and Bellevue are actually the same road, but the section around Graceland was later renamed in Presley's honor.

The Leonard's on Fox Plaza in the Fox Meadows neighborhood is the only location left. It opened in 1987, while the famed Bellevue restaurant closed in 1991 as business there diminished. "This neighborhood is perceived as dangerous, and though we do good lunch business, it has shrunk over the years," said Richard A. Jacobs (president of Leonard's Inc. at the time) during an interview with the *Commercial Appeal* published on May 20, 1991. "If you put it on a graph, it's steadily going down. Our lease runs out in August, and we've decided to leave before then."

In the article about the closing of the Bellevue location, General Manager Dan Brown, who currently owns Leonard's, described the cooking process. "You put down a bed of coals and four feet above the coals you put a grate. You put your meat on the grate and cook until it's done. That's it. There's no hocus-pocus about it and it hasn't changed in 60 years."

The remaining Leonard's still serves great sandwiches, like the ones Elvis Presley loved—assembled on a hot griddle to perfectly toast the buns. The dry ribs—with their charred, deliciously seasoned outer surface covering rich, smoky meat—are a more recent addition. Brown cooks them for roughly three and a half hours, while shoulders cook about eleven hours. The delicious rub added to the dry ribs is a surprisingly simple mixture of paprika, chili powder, garlic powder, black pepper and salt, according to Brown, who wouldn't reveal the magic ratios behind the rub.

Today, Leonard's still uses two old charcoal pits for ribs. Shoulders cook in a gas-fired Southern Pride cooker, but it is also loaded with a mix of charcoal and hickory. And at the end of the process, the shoulders are finished off in the charcoal pit to get a perfect bark on them. "The wood and the smoke from the charcoal puts the flavor to it," Brown said. To fire up the old pits, Brown said that he merely puts a bag of charcoal in them, bag and all, over some newspaper, lays some cardboard on top and lights it. After about an hour, the pit is ready for meat. The fat drippings that land on the coals add an unmatchable element of flavor, but they also make pit fires a constant danger.

Brown had a sprinkler system installed in his pits after one of them caught fire on Labor Day in 1996. On one of the busiest days in the barbecue business, he had to let an entire batch of shoulders burn up. "You can't open the door if it fires up," he explained. "A fireball will come out as big as the door and bounce across the room."

The Leonard's on Bellevue had outdoor pits where cooks could stand to the side and throw the pit doors open to release that giant fireball before calming the flames. That isn't possible in the crowded indoor kitchen at the Fox Plaza store, so the sprinklers are used to avoid the tragedy of standing in front of a sweltering pit door knowing that you are unable to do anything as a full load of meat burns to ruin.

Brown insists that a good barbecue restaurant has to cook every day it is open to maintain a consistent quality. "It doesn't go bad; it just loses its flavor. All that smoke flavor you spent all that time putting in there," he said.

The thick, hearty baked beans at Leonard's are Busch's Bean Pot baked beans with just two added ingredients: the restaurant's pulled pork and its "sweet sauce." Workers at the restaurant still refer to its signature barbecue sauce as "sweet sauce" because that is what Heuberger called it, although it isn't sugary tasting by the standards of today's sweet sauces. The sauce starts with a ketchup base that is cooked down with the "usual suspects" from the restaurant's dry rub, Brown said.

If imitation is the sincerest form of flattery, then it is interesting to note that a *Commercial Appeal* article from June 5, 1983, mentioned that John Willis, who won first place awards at Memphis in May in both 1980 and 1981, said that he made numerous trips to Leonard's while creating his own sauce. "I didn't copy Leonard's, but it was the taste I wanted," he said. Willis opened his own barbecue restaurant, John Willis Barbecue Pit, at 2450 Central in March 1983, just up the street from where Central BBQ is today.

Around the corner from the long-departed John Willis restaurant, the old Brady and Lil's recipes live on at the Bar-B-Q Shop, which has become as much of an institution for Midtown as Brady and Lil's was for South Memphis. Mondays are sauce day at the restaurant, when Eric Vernon makes a huge batch of sauce without any commonly used starters like ketchup or commercial base sauces. "We make our sauce completely from scratch," he said. "We start with a pot and some oil." There is a commercially prepared version of the sauce available in grocery stores under the name Dancing Pigs. The name came from customers who would look at the iconic pigs on the restaurant's T-shirts and sign and say, "Look at the dancing pigs." The commercial sauce is available in hot and mild, like the sauces in the restaurant. "When we put the Dancing Pig in the grocery stores, not a lot of people had a hot barbecue sauce," the thirty-nine-year-old Eric said. Its success quickly caused imitators to pop up.

Eric was a student at the University of Memphis, where he earned a MBA in marketing, when the family began selling the sauces in area grocery stores. "I'd get up, take my dad's Bronco and deliver to the back doors of Krogers, come here, work, then go to class." These days, the sauces are a big enough seller that they are kept in the Kroger warehouse and shipped to roughly one hundred stores in four states.

After growing up around the long hours and hectic pace of the restaurant business, Eric said that he pursued his MBA to get away from it. "I was absolutely not going to do this. I said, 'I'm just going to get me a business degree, and I'm going to do something different.'" But as he was finishing up his undergraduate degree in marketing management, his dad mentioned that he was also ready to step away from the restaurant. Eric still earned his MBA, but "I thought about it and thought, man, as much as this place has gotten on my nerves at times, I don't want it to go away. I can't tell you the countless families I've gotten close with. We see them on birthdays, graduations, engagements; they come in after funerals. It means a lot to a lot of people, and I appreciate that. I would miss my customers more than anything. A lot of my best friends I've met between these walls. It's a hard job, but when it's good it's great."

The Pig-N-Whistle and Gridley's names also survive with one remaining store apiece. The Kerrville location of Pig-N-Whistle, which opened in 2004, occupies a former general store constructed around 1800. The historic building sits next to train tracks in a setup similar to the Germantown Commissary.

The sixty-four-year-old current owner, Bill Rupert, spent his life working around the country in the restaurant business. He bought into Pig-N-Whistle in 1996 after helping advise a friend who opened the now-closed Bartlett location in 1990. The later locations were smaller than the original on Union, which represented a grandiose style of locally owned restaurant that faded away after the '60s, Rupert said. "The restaurant business changed after the '60s when the local places became more of the mom and pop places," he said.

Rupert uses a Southern Pride cooker loaded with pure hickory wood. "That's Memphis style. We never want to change that," he said. While some cooks believe in seasoning shoulders and basting them while they cook, Rupert believes in leaving them alone as much as possible. "Every time you open those pit doors, you change something in the meat. It's a process, and every time you open that door, you interrupt it." Using shoulders instead of butts is an important part of the process to him. "The best barbecue is in the shoulder. That's the only way to go. The skin holds juice in and bastes the meat. The fat tissue underneath the skin draws down into the meat. I didn't learn that overnight. To make good barbecue, you have to learn from your mistakes."

For ribs, he insists on St. Louis–cut spare ribs. He dusts them with his paprika-based rub before putting them in the pit and believes they are best served in the "muddy" style that combines rub sprinkled on top of sauce. "I think muddy is the way to go. It gives you the two tiers of flavor."

The ribs usually cook for about four and a half hours. Rupert checks them for doneness by picking them up with tongs and watching how they sag and where they begin to break apart. After cooking, they are wrapped before they are stored and then quickly heated for just a few minutes on a four-hundred-degree grill before serving them. "If it's on the grill three minutes, it's too much. What you do between the pit and the plate is what determines the experience for the person eating." Like Dan Brown at Leonard's, Rupert said that he considers it important to cook every day. "Old fat, after two days, it has an old fat flavor."

Meanwhile, after the sudden loss of patriarch Clyde Gridley, his family soldiered on, trying to run the business before it ended up in bankruptcy court. A group of investors headed by Jack Ivy and Bob Peterson bought it in the early '90s. By then, the original Summer Avenue location was gone, replaced by the Macon store and another on Winchester that had a takeout area separate from the main dining area, Ivy said.

To lower operating expenses, the new owners shut down the dine-in area of the Winchester store and began opening smaller locations around town. All the barbecue was initially cooked in the old charcoal pits at Winchester and delivered daily to the five satellite locations that were all branded Gridley's

II, Ivy said. Eventually gas-fired Southern Pride pits were added at the other locations before the partners, who were already retired when they entered the barbecue business, decided to sell. "We just got tired of it," Ivy said.

There were four Gridley's locations left when another retiree, former dentist Dr. Bill Coley, bought the one on Stage Road at Summer Avenue in 2003, while the former owners closed the other three. Coley bought the restaurant with fond memories of its heyday in the '70s. "Back in those days, it was the premier barbecue place other than Leonard's," he said.

Coley's daugher, Camille Duke, ran the Stage location during the brief period her family owned it. "Doug Walker came by and was interested in buying it," said the eighty-eight-year-old Coley, referring to the current owner. "I told him I wasn't interested in selling it. Three or four weeks later, I had a day where the air conditioning went out, the pit cook didn't show up and I said, 'I've had enough. I'm supposed to be retired.'"

Doug and his wife, Jamie Walker, bought the restaurant in October 2006 with a passion for food but no prior experience running a restaurant. Before then, they owned an industrial supply business in their hometown of Greenwood, Mississippi, in the Mississippi Delta. When that business was hammered by foreign competition, they turned to the restaurant industry. They trained on the job for a month before signing the papers, learning the recipes and how to run the pit from the employees, Jamie said.

Jamie had been a fan of Gridley's since she first visited the Summer location in the '70s. "After I had the barbecue shrimp one time, birthdays and anniversaries when my husband would ask what I wanted, I wanted to go to Gridley's. You might wait two hours, but you'd just sit back and talk to people."

Of the two restaurants Jack Whitaker founded in 1982, one has survived as a beloved neighborhood establishment, while the other, which stayed in the family, eventually closed when Whitaker's granddaughter tired of the exhausting grind of keeping it running.

Jack's Bar-B-Q Rib Shack closed in November 2013, after thirty-one years in business, when thirty-seven-year-old owner Sharon Whitaker, who started busing tables there when she was nine, stepped away to pursue a career in real estate property management. Her father, Jack Jr., had passed away in 2003, two years after he was initially diagnosed with ALS, commonly referred to as Lou Gehrig's disease. Sharon had been heavily involved in the restaurant's day-to-day operations for more than a decade by that point, since she was sixteen. But before his battle with ALS, Jack Jr. had handled the background details like bookkeeping and ordering. "I had a great dad. It's a horrible, horrible, horrible disease," she said of the debilitating condition that robs sufferers of all control over their bodies.

Sharon said that her mother had no interest in running the business, so she took over all aspects of it. She also had to adjust to a new cooking system when her brother Jack III, who owns R.J. Property Management, purchased the building and insisted that she remove the old steel behemoth of a charcoal pit and replace it with a modern gas-fired cooker from Ole Hickory. While the old pit created incredible barbecue, it was also a temperamental, fire-belching beast that caught the building on fire on several occasions, including a fire in the late '90s that kept the restaurant closed two weeks for repairs. Despite the great food Sharon created with it, Jack III wasn't willing to have the fire hazard in a building he owned, which included other tenants like the High Pockets pool hall next door to Jack's.

"It was a big adjustment for me. It probably took me a year to figure it out where the food would taste how I like. I thought I was going to run everybody away," Sharon said. The new cooker "was just a big metal box. It was totally unseasoned. You've gotta get some grease in there. But it's like anything else, once you learn it, it's science."

She burned hickory wood in the new cooker for smoke flavor. It removed the pressure of constantly tending to the pit since it had a thermostat to add gas heat anytime the fire dropped too low. It was still a tough period of transition. Another one of Sharon's four brothers, Joe Whitaker, moved to Memphis to help with the restaurant, but he passed away a year after their father around the same time Sharon was pregnant with her first child.

Sharon got some much-needed help from a regular customer who was a member at her family's church. Larry Mayes learned to cook barbecue from his brothers, who owned several Loeb's Bar-B-Q franchises in Arkansas. Mayes was a regular on the Memphis Barbecue Network (MBN) and Kansas City Barbeque Society (KCBS) competition circuits. In 1999, he competed in the whole hog category in eighteen MBN events. He took first place in seventeen of them, including Memphis in May, and second place in the remaining one. His large trophy collection also includes a 2000 first-place award for sauce from the prestigious Jack Daniel's World Championship Invitational Barbecue Competition.

When Mayes began working with Sharon in 2004, he brought a wealth of knowledge and a new menu item. "In KCBS [competitions], you had to cook brisket if you wanted to be grand champion," Mayes explained. Brisket is frequently the cut of choice for barbecue west of the Mississippi River, where land was better suited to cattle. Teams competing in KCBS have to turn in meats in four categories: pork shoulder, chicken, pork ribs and beef brisket. Mayes, a Memphis native who has also lived in Texas and Kansas City, won first-place awards in KCBS competitions with his brisket and taught Sharon his technique.

In 2008, Mayes opened his own restaurant, Fat Larry's, farther east on Summer Avenue after he failed to talk Sharon into moving Jack's Rib Shack to a more affluent area. Fat Larry's offers southern plate lunches with foods like country-fried steak and turnip greens along with barbecue. "I just wasn't interested," Sharon said of her decision to keep Jack's at its original location. "I was where I already felt safe and had a lot of repeat customers."

The one constant helper Sharon had throughout her time at the restaurant was Robert Johnston, who went to work there just a year after Jack's opened at the age of eighteen. "He was one of the main reasons I didn't want to close," she said. Sharon and Johnston both had homes near the restaurant and would trade off the duties of putting shoulders in the cooker at night, coming in to put ribs on at 7:00 a.m., coming back at 9:00 a.m. to prepare to open for lunch at 11:00 a.m., closing at 11:00 p.m. and then restarting the entire process. Meanwhile, without her father to handle the bookkeeping, Sharon spent a decade dealing with all the headaches associated with business taxes and licenses.

Although she ultimately decided to escape from the constant grind, closing the doors for good was a bittersweet experience. While she was excited about her fresh start in the real estate business, the Rib Shack represented a lifetime of memories for her. "It is so weird not working in a restaurant," she said. "The customers are what I really miss now. A lot of them knew me personally and had watched me grow up since I was six years old."

Over at the Three Little Pigs, owner Charlie Robertson didn't want to mess with success, but success forced one change. In 1995, he had to switch from the old Loeb's charcoal pit to a modern gas-assisted pit from Ole Hickory, "primarily because our pit was not big enough." The new pit could handle forty shoulders compared to the old one's max of sixteen.

As the name implies, the initial fire in a gas-fired pit is lit by a gas flame, and it can be used as a conventional gas oven. Because of that, a lot of bad barbecue has been cooked with them, causing many purists to be dismissive of them. But Robertson stressed that he keeps his firebox filled with wood. "Once you add the hickory to it and that chamber fills with smoke, you get that good flavor," he said.

In fact, the new pit helped Robertson improve consistency while reducing waste. "If [the charcoal pit] flashes and catches fire, everything has that

The Three Little Pigs at Quince and White Station is as close as modern Memphians can get to the experience of dining at a Loeb's Bar-B-Q. The restaurant still has the departed chain's signature pig sign and still uses recipes handed down by deceased former Loeb's franchise owner and longtime Three Little Pigs employee Helen McClendon.

singed, burned flavor," he said. The charcoal pits the Loeb's restaurants used kept meat on grates about four feet above the coals. They require constant attention, and the flame is heavily influenced by outside factors like wind around the chimney. When everything is perfect with a charcoal pit, the barbecue that comes out of them is unbeatable, "but that only happened about three days a week," Robertson said.

Even when everything went perfect, the old pit didn't yield as much usable meat per shoulder, he added. An eighteen-pound shoulder would cook down to ten or eleven pounds compared to twelve pounds on the Ole Hickory pit. He goes through 100 to 150 shoulders per week, so an extra pound per shoulder adds up to more than five thousand pounds of extra meat in a year. For a place selling a regular barbecue sandwich for $3.29, that represents a significant boost to the bottom line.

While most restaurants cite cook times in the neighborhood of twelve hours for shoulders and butts, Robertson said that he cooks his for more than twenty hours with no rub or other preparation. "It goes straight into the pit, nothing but smoke. We don't do anything but lay it in there and leave it alone—give it plenty of time and plenty of smoke," he said.

The Three Little Pigs initially had plate-glass exterior walls surrounding the dining room like all the old Loeb's Bar-B-Q restaurants. Robertson replaced them with solid walls in the late '90s to give the air conditioner a fighting chance in the summertime, since the building is surrounded by a giant blacktop parking lot.

One thing that hasn't changed in decades is that nearly every available inch of wall space in the Three Little Pigs restaurant is devoted to pig images, statues and figurines. The pigs started showing up shortly after Robertson took over. Someone gave him a ceramic pig, and he set it out in the dining room. Customers began buying pigs to donate anywhere they encountered them. He has figurines from everywhere from England to Africa. The collection is now too big to display everything. "I've got boxes of them in storage," he said. Keeping them clean with the dust and grease created by a busy restaurant is a steady chore that has tempted him to get rid of them at times, but he said he can never bring himself to do it.

The customer devotion to providing for the little restaurant also extends to the woodpile outside. The surrounding neighborhood is full of hickory trees, and Robertson said that customers call whenever a tree goes down to see if he needs wood. It's the kind of friendship between a restaurant and its customers that is unique to locally owned neighborhood joints. "It's a good little place, but you have to watch it," Robertson said.

The same year that the Three Little Pigs was transitioning to its gas-assisted cooker, another old name in Memphis barbecue was finding new life with a new owner. Tom's Bar-B-Q and Deli is at the corner of Getwell and Raines. The restaurant sits in between the airport, which is home to major hubs for both FedEx and UPS, and the enormous railroad switchyard that stretches from Perkins to Shelby Drive along Lamar Avenue. The area in between is largely devoted to the logistics industry—the business of getting goods from their point of origin to their point of consumption as efficiently as possible. The small army of people that works in that field frequently heads to Tom's for lunch because it operates like a well-oiled machine in the world of barbecue logistics.

If you stop at Tom's during the lunch rush, don't let the long line snaking through the labyrinth of a building frighten you. "We're always known for our fast service," said owner Adam Itayem, who bought the restaurant from its founder, Tom Sturgius, back in 1995. "You shouldn't be waiting more than five minutes."

While Loeb's Bar-B-Q is long gone, the old pig-shaped signs are still sprinkled throughout the city, like this one in front of a former Loeb's that later served as a soul food restaurant on South 3rd Street. The sign in front of the Three Little Pigs at Quince and White Station is the only one with the pig painting preserved. Others, like the red sign in front of Bryant's Breakfast on Summer, have been repainted to disguise them over the years.

The restaurant expanded numerous times throughout its more than fifty years in business, creating a network of enclosed former patios that surround the original kitchen like rings in a tree trunk. When Itayem bought it, the entire building consisted of just the little order area and the part of the kitchen behind it. At the time, there were just three ladies working the counter, and while the lines were long, the waits were too. Now ten employees work as a well-choreographed team, putting orders together with practiced speed. During the week, the restaurant regularly serves 1,500 to 2,000 customers per day Itayem said.

Sturgius was a Greek immigrant, and like the famous Rendezvous restaurant downtown, the seasoning at Tom's bears a heavy Greek influence. Itayem, who was born inside the Old City walls of Jerusalem and immigrated to the United States when he was four, was no stranger to Mediterranean spices when he took over. He hasn't altered the original rub recipe, which includes chili powder, paprika, salt, black pepper, thyme, oregano, pickling spice, celery salt, garlic salt, red pepper and nutmeg. Meat is coated with the rub and allowed to marinate in the moisture it draws out for up to forty-eight hours before going into the pit.

That old charcoal pit is crucial to the flavor profile, Itayem said. "The drippings getting on the coals and the smoke from them coming back up on the meat is part of the flavor, and you can't re-create that," he said. Salespeople have taken him to try gas-fired pits and tried to convince him to modernize his operation. "It's convenient. It's fast. But that's cheating to me. It's more personal when we do it this way."

The sauces are also made in-store with plenty of the rub as a primary ingredient. Along with a standard mild sauce, Tom's also has a sweet and spicy jalapeño sauce that offers a little more kick, along with a habanero sauce that is fiery hot. At a place so focused on speed, you might expect an abbreviated menu, but Tom's offers spare and baby back ribs, its famous rib tips, chopped pork, brisket, chicken, turkey and barbecue bologna, which Itayem calls "Tennessee round steak," as well as deli foods and fried catfish.

Itayem said that he uses shoulders for his chopped pork because Boston butt doesn't have a long-enough shelf life since the leaner, skinless meat dries out so quickly. Describing his approach to brisket, he said, "It's not Texas style. It's more Mediterranean style." If there is one item on the menu that best represents that Mediterranean influence, it's the rib tips. Unlike most rib tips, his are made from a riblet cut from the upper loin area and are grilled in the lower portion of the pit like ribs at the Rendezvous instead of being cooked with indirect heat like traditional barbecue.

CHAPTER 9

COMPETITION

B y the turn of the millennium, the Memphis in May barbecue festival had evolved into its current state, which Jimmy Ogle described as "our cross between Mardi Gras and Halloween," following a 1991 expansion of Tom Lee Park. The city raised Riverside Drive and stabilized the Bluff while increasing the size of the park from eight acres to thirty.

The event is now officially called the Memphis in May World Championship Barbecue Cooking Contest, but most Memphians just refer to it as Barbecue Fest. For most locals, it is Spring Break for grown-ups, but for dedicated competitors, it is one of the most prestigious competitions in the country alongside the Royal Invitational in Kansas City and the Jack Daniel's Invitational in Lynchburg, Tennessee.

It has become a truly international event, drawing people from around the world. In 1987, the *Commercial Appeal* told the story of one foreign team that took high honors after famed Memphian Thomas "Silky" Sullivan decided to introduce Ireland to American barbecue in 1984. Sullivan owned the Silky O' Sullivan's restaurant and bar that started life in Overton Square during the Square's original heyday before relocating to Beale as that street began its dramatic turnaround. A fun-loving character who passed away in 2013 at the age of seventy-one, he once chartered a plane and took twenty-five barrel cookers to Ireland.

"I had to bring it over," the *Commercial Appeal* quoted him as saying on August 19, 1987. "When those cookers rolled off the plane, the Irish didn't know what to think. They thought they were some kind of bombs. They all jumped

The view of the Mississippi River and the Hernando de Soto Bridge from Tom Lee Park during the 1984 Memphis in May barbecue competition. *Courtesy of the Memphis and Shelby County Room, Memphis Public Library.*

back." A few years after the first Irish Cup Invitational Barbecue Festival, the Irish had embraced Memphis barbecue thoroughly enough for an Irish team, appropriately called the Irish Team, to take first place in ribs at the 1987 Memphis in May competition. "In less than three years the Irish have gone from knowing nothing about barbecue to being gourmets," Sullivan boasted.

Today, the Memphis in May contest draws more than 250 teams and 100,000 visitors to the now mile-long park next to the Mississippi River every year. Ribs, shoulder and whole hog are the official categories the booths are divided into around the park, but they can all be divided into three additional categories.

There are hobbyist booths. Competing at Memphis in May is expensive, so these booths normally have a few dedicated barbecue cooks on the team along with a bunch of friends who are there to lend a hand, pitch in money and enjoy the massive party. They are cooking good food, but they are under no illusion that they are going to win big.

James Rudolph freely admits that his team is more of a hobbyist team. "We're not expecting to win Memphis in May, but we've had some decent success. We're focused more on the core members having a good time," he said. His Pork University team has finished as high as thirteenth place in shoulder.

Rudolph started Pork University with friends from college shortly after he graduated in 2005, but barbecue has been in his blood his entire life. "Our family on my mom's side, they have smoke pits," he said. "We've been doing it since the '40s." Rudolph's parents, William and Linda Rudolph, still have a pit in the backyard at their Clarksville, Tennessee home, and the two of them always attend the Memphis in May contest to assist their son.

Rudolph cooks with a combination of lump charcoal and hickory and mesquite wood and competes in both the Kansas City Barbeque Society and Memphis Barbecue Network circuits. He settled on those woods mainly due to the fact that they are generally available anywhere he cooks, which helps him maintain consistency. He said that he enjoys the blind judging aspect of KCBS competitions and feels like money can sometimes have too much of an influence in MBN competitions, where presentation is part of the grading.

He started the team with fellow Sigma Phi Epsilon fraternity alumni from the University of Memphis so they and their friends and family could fully experience the Memphis in May event. "If you don't know anyone with a team, you're just walking around watching everyone else have a good time," Rudolph said.

Rudolph originally purchased his competition cooker for tailgating at University of Memphis football games. He still relies on tailgate parties for tweaking recipes and techniques. He saw the cooker listed on eBay and drove to Savannah, Georgia, to pick it up. "It was perfect for our purposes," he said. "I drove down to Savannah on a Thursday morning and got back just in time to tailgate on Saturday. I pulled in, dropped it off and we were off to the races."

Money separates the corporate booths from the hobbyist teams. It's impossible to gauge the real impact of Barbecue Fest on the local economy because there is no way of calculating just how many deals are born out of the networking that occurs there. Like in other cities, the golf course is an important place for deal-making in Memphis. But there are plenty of important connections made over ribs and beer next to the Mississippi River in May. Businesses spend piles of money putting up elaborate multilevel booths with professional DJs, bartenders and mountains of food. Getting into those booths generally requires a wristband, which requires a connection to whomever is writing the check.

Competing in Memphis in May requires such a big investment in hard work and money that even hobbyist teams seek corporate sponsorship money where they can find it. Michael Cerrito helped organize and cook for the Trailer Pork team that competed from 2004 through 2008. The team still competes occasionally at smaller MBN competitions, but the hassle of the big competition became too much as members of the team began getting married and having children.

The Trailer Pork team usually had a budget of about $10,000, which required annual dues of up to $450 per member depending on how much additional corporate sponsorship the team could drum up. Cerrito noted, "Those twenty-plus people each want to bring their five best friends. A sponsor can be a mixed blessing because you're basically selling one night to the person who writes the check for them to use the booth for their guests."

"When we started, we were all in our early thirties," said the forty-year-old Cerrito. "You get kind of burned out. It all comes down to money and time and intestinal fortitude." The twenty-five-member team had four head cooks, including Cerrito, while other members primarily helped with tasks like loading equipment in and out, manning the booth's entrance, cleaning up and going on beer and ice runs.

The team finished as high as twenty-eighth place in ribs, which is a good showing in a field as crowded and competitive as the rib category at Memphis in May. "Looking at the score cards, the difference between the score at twenty-eighth place and the score at first is so minute it's ridiculous," Cerrito said.

Despite the fun, the week wears on teams as it progresses. "Everybody's ready to go at load-in on Sunday. Load-out the next Sunday is a giant pain. You're hung over, you're tired and if people don't carry their weight, it's bothersome. You end up saying, 'We could've done this in five minutes if you guys showed.' Even if you've done it five years in a row, there's still a year-to-year team maintenance you have to do. Stuff gets tore up."

The Trailer Pork team walked the line between the hobbyist booths and the big corporate booths. Both are largely centered on eating, drinking and having a good time. Meanwhile, the people at the serious competitor booths are there to win. They are smaller teams displaying impressive assortments of trophies from previous barbecue competitions. Some of the teams still party while they work, while others are all business. Either way, they are there because they are dedicated to the craft of slow-cooked pork and want to flex their skills for the big-money prizes.

Whether hobbyists or serious contenders, teams with a true passion for barbecue spend the rest of the year traveling to smaller competitions in either the KCBS or the MBN circuits. The competitions are usually held in small towns and hosted by other organizations. "We're just there to verify the integrity of the event," said MBN vice-president and founding member Suzanne Rhea. The founders were five couples who were all Memphis in May–certified judges when Memphis in May decided to drop its circuit to focus on the big annual event in Memphis around 2005, Rhea said.

"We were passionate about barbecue. We have all made lots of great friends through it, and we didn't want to see the Memphis circuit competitions go away," she said. The MBN uses the same judging format as Memphis in May, with whole hog, ribs and shoulder as the three primary categories and separate rounds of blind and on-site judging, but teams can enter in as many of they categories as they want. The judges in the blind area still rate the appearance of the meat; they just don't know where it came from. During the on-site visits, teams explain their cooking process and the woods, temperatures and seasonings they use.

"They have to put on a little show. Every team starts with a ten. That's a perfect score," Rhea said. Judges drop that perfect score by fractional points as they rate the food. "What we're looking for is the best product there today. A lot of times it's very minor differences that determine the winner."

Teams are judged on the appearance of the entry, taste and tenderness and overall impression. Rhea stressed that mushy, "fall off the bone" meat that ends up with what she described as a "peanut butter–like mouth feel" is not considered ideal. It needs to be tender but still maintain a meaty texture and "pull." MBN is the only all-pork barbecue network in the country. "I think whole hog is what truly distinguishes us from other networks," Rhea said. "It's the hardest to cook." For whole hog, judges sample meat from the shoulder, loin and ham areas of the hog to make sure the front, middle and back are all cooked correctly.

Like at Memphis in May, for the final round the judges resample the top entries to determine the first-, second- and third-place winner in each category. The grand championship is awarded to whichever team scores the highest overall in any of the three categories. "The grand champion is the best product on the park today," Rhea said.

Central BBQ owners Craig Blondis and Roger Sapp both competed in the barbecue circuit, with Blondis on the Redeye Smokers team and Sapps on the Hogaholics team. The two met while Blondis was bartending at the Poplar Lounge, a Midtown-area bar that served as the setting for the club run by Isaac Hayes's character in the movie *Hustle & Flow*. Both men played soccer, and that, combined with their love of barbecue, led to them becoming friends, Blondis said.

They opened their first location on Central near the University of Memphis in April 2002. The relative newcomer to the local barbecue scene, which now has three locations, quickly amassed an impressive number of first-place awards in local barbecue restaurant rankings. The ribs pack a good dry rub over a tastily charred outer surface and a delicious pink interior. The lines can be long, especially at the original location, but like at Tom's, the friendly crew maintains a frantic pace to keep it steadily moving.

The restaurant started when Sapps sold a four-plex rental property he owned and needed to quickly reinvest the money to avoid capital gains taxes, Blondis said. The Central Avenue property he purchased had been home to enough failed restaurants that business professors at the nearby University of Memphis used it as an example of a "kiss of death location." Previous businesses had focused their attention on beer bust nights to bring in college students, a business model that only brought in crowds on drink special nights, and those crowds were specifically there to hang out without spending much. Blondis said that he and Sapps brainstormed and decided to open a barbecue restaurant. By then, Blondis had experience managing two locations of the old Pig-N-Whistle barbecue chain, while Sapps had retired from his career as an accounting comptroller, giving the new venture experts for both the food and money side of the business.

Since previous businesses at the Central location had all failed trying to rely on beer sales to broke college students, Blondis said that he and Sapps wanted to intentionally avoid crowds of people sipping beers on the Central Avenue restaurant's spacious front patio in order to keep tables open and maintain the food volume they needed to be profitable. Central sells an impressive variety of local microbrews, but there is no table service, so anyone wanting a second will have to go back through the line.

"We pretty much took the competitive-style barbecue and brought it to the public," Blondis said. "Basically we opened this business on $50,000. Roger maxed out his AmEx card, and that's how we started." The name of the business came from Memphis's location in the middle of barbecue country, as well as the street on which it is located. That mentality is echoed in Central's four sauces.

"If you cook barbecue properly, you don't need any sauce. It's supposed to be an accompaniment," Blondis said. Before opening the original restaurant, he and Sapps had a party where they offered about ten different sauces and had guests fill out cards to rate them. The top four from that experiment are the four served to this day.

The most popular sauce, the mild, is a traditional Memphis-/Kansas City–style tomato sauce with plenty of molasses and brown sugar. The hot, which is great with the restaurant's pulled pork, is a Texas-influenced bourbon and Tabasco sauce. The mustard sauce is a style common along the East Coast from South Carolina down into Florida. The ultra-runny vinegar sauce is heavily influenced by the sauces found in North Carolina and Kentucky. The vinegar sauce is good for dipping the meat from Central's ribs, and Blondis said that he reduces it by 50 percent and uses it as a finishing sauce for ribs when he competes.

Sourcing hardwood is normally a chore for barbecue restaurants, but Central was barely open for a year when it got a literal windfall of wood when the gigantic summer storm nicknamed Hurricane Elvis slammed the Memphis area during July 2013. Straight-line winds moving over the Mississippi River at more than one hundred miles per hour created what then Shelby County mayor A.C. Wharton referred to as a "dry land hurricane" that crushed buildings, uprooted trees and left 70 percent of the county without power. It also left Central with an enormous pile of hickory and pecan, the two woods used in the gas-fired Ole Hickory cooker at Central, Blondis said.

The success of the first restaurant caused Blondis and Sapps to buy a second building in downtown's South Main District. That building was previously owned by the Drake Sandwich Company, which produced premade sandwiches for convenience stores. Although it was in a neighborhood seeing rapid revitalization, the building needed to be completely remodeled to be a barbecue restaurant.

Before starting work on the South Main building, the partners got an opportunity to quickly open a second location when a Red Lobster on Summer Avenue near Perkins closed, and its building went on the market. "Garden Entertainment—who owns Red Lobster—when they sell their buildings, they don't gut them. We just had to put the smokers in, and we were ready to go," Blondis said.

The cavernous Summer location took a lot of strain off the much smaller original location when it opened in 2006. "This entire restaurant would fit in the kitchen at Summer," Blondis said during an interview at the Central location. The new location had a maximum capacity of 220 people, compared to 50 on Central.

Blondis's wife, Elizabeth, quit her job as a paralegal to join the company during the same period following the birth of the couple's first child. The fifty-one-year-old Craig Blondis said that he got married the same month the original location on Central opened. "The first couple years, we didn't see much of each other. The first five years, I was here from open to close pretty much every day. I'd sleep in the back of my truck during the day to get some rest."

Now Elizabeth handles the company's shipping and catering business from the Summer Avenue location, while Craig has built up a management team he can rely on. "It took a lot for me to trust somebody else with my business," he said. He now has people on his staff who have been with him for over a decade of his twelve years in business. "If you take care of your employees and treat them the way you'd want to be treated, they'll watch

The downtown location of Central BBQ sits directly down the hill from the former Lorraine Motel, which is now home to the National Civil Rights Museum in the revitalized South Main District. The exterior of the motel building, including the balcony where Dr. Martin Luther King Jr. was assassinated, and the room King stayed in are restored and preserved to reflect their condition on that tragic day.

your back." He still maintains a watchful eye on his kitchens though. He said that by noon most days, he has hit all three locations at least twice.

For the third location, Blondis and Sapps completely overhauled the old sandwich building near South Main. "That was the first time we were able to put our own footprint on a location," Blondis said. It opened in October 2012, but the work there isn't complete. The restaurant is in the process of adding a large covered patio, like the one on Central, but with an outdoor cooking area for classes and demonstrations. The South Main location opened less than a year after the Double J Smokehouse, another downtown barbecue joint just half a block away. The two restaurants created a welcomed off-Beale zone for real Memphis barbecue aimed more at locals than tourists.

While Blondis said that he and Sapps would like to expand further, their top priority is maintaining consistency. "If you put out a good product and you're consistent, people will come back to you," he said. "Our growth plan is to open one every three to five years."

CHAPTER 10
FAME AND FORTUNE

Of the brands that rose up in the '80s, Jim Neely's Interstate Bar-B-Q and Corky's have become the most famous even beyond Memphis. Interstate's success turned barbecue into a family craft for the Neelys. Jim Neely's wife still works with him in the original restaurant, while their youngest son, Keith, manages the Southaven, Mississippi location. Their middle son, Ken, is back at the main location after a brief foray running his own place called Ken Neely's Bar-B-Q in Hickory Hill. And most famously, Jim Neely's nephew, Patrick Neely, learned to cook barbecue at Interstate before opening his own Neely's Bar-B-Q branded restaurants in Memphis that led to he and his wife, Gina, starring in the Food Network series *Down Home with the Neelys*.

Patrick Neely's restaurants were reliable Memphis favorites for years, but when the time demands of the show turned the couple into absentee owners, there was a noticeable drop in quality and service that made it unsurprising when they closed. It doesn't matter how famous your name is, Memphians are serious about barbecue, and it doesn't take many experiences with dirty restaurants, inattentive service and ribs that taste like they were cooked in a gas-only oven for locals to give up on a place. Jim Neely continues to steadfastly watch over his own establishment, and he didn't mince any words talking about the demise of his nephew's restaurants. "It dropped off bad because Pat wasn't there. He was running up and down the country playing celebrity chef," he said. "They got egotistical. That's why they're not in business anymore."

Patrick's brother, Tony Neely, is currently working to renovate and reopen the old downtown location of Neely's Bar-B-Q on Jefferson near the historic mansions of Victorian Village. Other relatives also learned barbecue from Jim Neely and have gone on to run restaurants in other states. He said that their individual success or failure depends on their commitment to consistency. "In the food business, the product is only as good as the owner," he said.

Corky's is probably the most nationally famous name in Memphis barbecue. In addition to the original location, the company began expanding with a Germantown Road restaurant in 1998. Since then, it has added additional stores in Collierville and Olive Branch, Mississippi. There are also franchise locations in Little Rock, Arkansas; New Orleans, Louisiana; Gatlinburg, Tennessee; Pigeon Forge, Tennessee; and Brentwood, Tennessee. And the company has a huge presence for its precooked frozen ribs in grocery stores and on the QVC shopping channel.

The ribs shipped to grocery stores and QVC customers are cooked in five huge Southern Pride cookers at a USDA-approved commercial kitchen in the Bellbrook Industrial Park on Brooks Road near Elvis Presley Boulevard. The company took over a nine-thousand-square-foot kitchen space left vacant when the Schnuck's grocery chain acquired the old Memphis-area Seessel's stores. Since then, the commercial kitchen has expanded to seventy thousand square feet.

At its current size, the USDA kitchen can cook six thousand slabs of ribs and five thousand butts per day, according to the kitchen's general manager Joel Storck. It uses Boston butts instead of the shoulders used in the restaurant since they have a higher yield and are broken down into meal portions and frozen as soon as they are cooked. The skin and extra fat on shoulders that help protect the meat from drying as it is pulled to order in the restaurants would just be added waste in the commercial kitchen.

While the ribs at the restaurants are prepared in charcoal-fired pits, the USDA kitchen uses gas cookers to handle the volume of ribs that pass through it while meeting all the namesake USDA regulations required for packaged foods. Hickory wood burns in the gas flame for smoke flavor.

Even in a factory-like setting, barbecue is an art that resists standardization. "All those cookers cook a little differently," Storck said. Ribs and butts vary in size and fat content, while the hickory logs vary in size, age, dryness and specific variety of hickory. Outside changes in the weather affect cooking times the same way they do for small competition barbecue teams with portable cookers. The meat still requires an experienced eye for when it is

The burn chamber in a modern gas-fired Ole Hickory cooker at the Corky's USDA commercial kitchen. Wood is set in the path of the gas flame to create smoke that feeds into the vents at the top of the cylinder.

Cooked and frozen Corky's ribs destined for grocery store and QVC customers are boxed on an assembly line at the Corky's USDA commercial kitchen in the Bellbrook Industrial Park.

ready instead of an automated timer. "That's what makes barbecue fun," said the forty-eight-year-old Storck, who began working for Corky's as a waiter in 1987, fell in love with the business and was promoted to managing the USDA kitchen in 1995.

While the packaged Corky's ribs come vacuum-sealed with a coating of sauce on them, the charcoal-cooked ribs in the restaurant are available either wet or with a delicious paprika-based dry rub and are notably better than their grocery store brethren. The restaurants also offer a brown ale on draft specifically crafted by the Abita brewery in Louisiana to pair with the dry ribs.

A new Olive Branch, Mississippi, location on Goodman Road represents the end of the company's plans for Memphis-area expansion, Barry Pelts said. It is also the first store that the Pelts built from the ground up instead of repurposing an existing building. "Opening that restaurant will be bittersweet," he said. Although Donald Pelts was technically retired when planning for the Olive Branch store began, he still made the deal for the land, picked the architect and helped pick the builder for the store—the first in the Memphis area with patio seating.

Donald Pelts passed away suddenly on May 15, 2013. It was the opening day of the Memphis in May barbecue contest and the same day that multiple-time Memphis in May grand champion John Willingham died. The two deaths came suddenly enough that Barry Pelts said that he and his father ran into Willingham days before while having lunch at the Perkins restaurant near the Poplar Avenue Corky's. The two barbecue icons talked and laughed.

Barry Pelts said that his father was active, doing the things he loved with no sign of health problems until the moment of his death. He spent four hours on his hands and knees helping Barry change tabletops in the restaurant before meeting a group of his best friends at their bridge club. It was also the night that the Memphis Grizzlies defeated the Oklahoma City Thunder to advance to the Western Conference Finals of the 2013 NBA playoffs. Donald, an avid Grizzlies fan, called his son to tell him he would swing by in ten minutes to watch the end of the game with him. When the phone rang ten minutes later, "I thought he was calling to say he was outside," Barry said. Instead, it was members of the bridge club calling to tell him that his father had passed away suddenly from a massive heart attack.

"He wasn't just my dad. He was my best friend and mentor too," Barry Pelts said. He shared a large office with his father, who consulted him constantly despite claims of being retired. Today, Barry runs the business with his brother-in-law, Andy Woodman, who joined the company as a partner in 1998.

Headed into the 2013 Memphis in May festival, the eighty-year-old John Willingham had experienced scares with heart disease in the past, but that year's competition represented another personal triumph for him. He had always been disappointed by health regulations that kept teams from selling barbecue to the general public so everyone could experience it. "That was his love," said Marge Willingham, his wife of fifty-seven years. "He loved Memphis. He always just wanted to make it better. His attitude was the most positive of anyone you'd ever meet. In all our years of married life, he never came home when he wasn't singing or whistling or humming. He wanted barbecue to be family oriented."

In 2013, he'd finally worked out a plan to sell barbecue from his contest site, which he visited the Friday before the competition to make preparations. "He wasn't feeling well, and I knew he wasn't feeling well. He didn't complain. You wouldn't have known," Marge said. "But he told me, 'I have to do it for the good of barbecue.'"

Marge said that she frequently asked John to slow down and retire to Florida, but he would always look at the Memphis landscape around him and ask, "What could be more beautiful than this day?" When John arrived home that Friday night, he only took a few bites of his dinner. He never left the house that weekend, lying down sick and coughing blood. "We didn't talk about it, but we knew his end was there," Marge said. He opted to stay home as long as possible, and although friends and relatives later asked why she didn't rush him to the hospital, Marge explained, "He wanted to be home. He loved our house and the view from the windows. He did not want to be at the hospital."

John ultimately did go to St. Francis Hospital, where he spent his final hours being held by his wife before he passed away on Wednesday night, May 15, 2013, around 6:00 p.m. during the opening of the Memphis in May contest. "He died strong. He died just how he lived," Marge said, struggling with tears.

The Willingham's World Champion Barbecue River City Rooters team was devastated by the news of John's passing but had to push on to achieve his dream of competing while selling to the public. "To be able to vend and be able to compete is an atrocious undertaking," team member Mike Simpson said. The team had to work from two adjoining but partitioned sites using separate cookers, with one side competing and the other vending, to meet health department regulations. "We as a team had to continue because it is what John would have wanted. We had to keep pushing on because it was happening."

Simpson is a retired fireman and the owner of Quality Stoves on South 3rd Street, where competition-level barbecue rigs are one of his offerings. In 1995, he helped John refine his Turbo Cooker from the early black, hot-rolled steel version to the final stainless steel rendition. "He was a one-of-a-kind man, always and forever discussing ideas and concepts," Simpson said. "He loved barbecue. He loved meeting people."

John Willingham's funeral was held on Sunday, May 19, 2013. It was both his eighty-first birthday and the day after the final awards ceremony for the 2013 Memphis in May barbecue contest.

At the 2013 Memphis in May awards ceremony, the twelve-member Sweet Swine O' Mine team took home the grand championship and first place in shoulder. "It was a dogfight," said dentist Dr. Richard Lackie, who serves as the team's "rib and sauce guy," of the 2013 finals. "We had three former champions in shoulder and a two-time champion in whole hog."

The Sweet Swine O' Mine team won its first grand championship in 2009 and has taken home the first-place trophy in shoulder four times. "The first time is excitement. It's pure joy," Lackie said. "The second time is validation and contentment."

Team member Blake Marcum was originally on a separate team, Too Sauced to Pork, that he helped found in 2005 before being invited to join Sweet Swine O' Mine for 2013. Marcum won second place in tomato-based sauce with his previous team at Memphis in May in 2012. The event features ancillary competitions for categories like tomato sauce, vinegar sauce, hot wings and anything but pork. Lackie said that when his team walked on stage to claim the 2013 grand championship trophy, he turned to Marcum and said, "Just soak it in. It's never the same."

"I have never felt that feeling before in my life," Marcum said. "I will always want to do that again. I was like a little school child. I was the first one up on stage. There was no stopping me. I had been up on stage before for side categories like sauce and hot wings, but that was my first time for a big product and it was a grand championship. It's your passion, your hobby; you just had your dreams come true."

Marcum's early days in competition barbecue were less successful. When he and former roommate Neil Gallagher formed Too Sauced to Pork under its original moniker of Swinebucks, their first competition was a MBN event in Wynn, Arkansas. "We just kind of realized we didn't know what we were doing at all," Marcum said. The team was initially sponsored by Starbucks, where Gallagher was a manager, and used a rub that was about 40 percent ground coffee with a sauce that was about 60 percent brewed coffee.

Since its inception, that team, which is still operated by Gallagher as Too Sauced to Pork, has kept its membership open to anyone who wants to join. "When we started, I told him my biggest problem I had with barbecue was it was too exclusive," Marcum said. This was before Memphis in May added activities like the Kingsford Tour of Champions, which allows spectators to judge entries, and the Cooker's Caravan, which provides a tour of team booths throughout the park. When Marcum and Gallagher were getting started, selling the opportunity to cook in the ancillary categories was a major source of funding for the team. It still welcomes new members to join on its website. In 2013, it featured members from twenty-two states and seven countries.

Marcum said that the team did well with on-site judges, when they could explain the dark color and unique flavor of the meat. "But our blind boxes would just get destroyed." In the meantime, Marcum continued to develop his own tomato sauce, and at an event where Gallagher ended up sick and unable to compete, Marcum decided to use it instead. "We jumped from finishing around eightieth place to twenty-fifth, and we said, 'Okay, this is the direction we want to go instead.'"

While Too Sauced tries to stay as inclusive as possible, membership on Sweet Swine O' Mine is invitation-only and requires unanimous agreement from the team. The thirty-four-year-old Marcum was the first new member added in three years, Lackie said. The team had already decided to invite him on before his 2012 sauce trophy. When adding new members, the team looks for the right combination of temperament, personality and work ethic.

Marcum said that too many people expect a step-by-step guide to making perfect barbecue on their first attempt. "I could give someone an exact, step-by-step recipe to what we do, and if they didn't have experience, they could completely mess it up. You've gotta go out there and fail. You've gotta go out on the porch and just cook."

Lackie said that Sweet Swine O' Mine uses the same basic approach for shoulders, ribs and whole hog. "We like to cook our products at 225 to 250 degrees." The team cooks with a mix of charcoal and a 3:2 mix of hickory and fruitwood. Hickory is a constant because it is such a signature element of Memphis barbecue flavor, but fruitwood helps avoid the bitterness that can result from using too much hickory. Apple is the team's fruitwood of choice.

While the wood is used for smoke, charcoal is always the primary heat source. Wood smoke is only used for the first third of the cook to "get that flavor in early and quick," Lackie said. He used to rely on lump charcoal but switched to briquettes as high-quality pure-hardwood briquettes with no binding agents became readily available. The team adamantly believes in a slow-and-low approach—cooking ribs for roughly six and a half hours, shoulders for eighteen hours and whole hogs for twenty-one to twenty-four hours. None of those times is set in stone.

"The worst mistake you can make with barbecue is having too much of a set schedule," Lackie said. "You have to know how to punt." Factors like wind, rain and outside temperature and humidity can all force quick decisions to remove wood, increase or decrease heat or apply foil wrap early.

The color of the meat indicates when it has absorbed enough smoke. Too much smoke can result in a processed meat flavor similar to a hot dog, Lackie said. The team uses the traditional Memphis approach of rubbing down meat with yellow mustard as an adhesive for dry rub on its raw shoulders and whole hogs, but it has abandoned that approach for ribs, where Lackie feels that it leaves the ribs a little too wet. With the shorter cook time for ribs, Lackie said that rub falling off during the cooking process isn't a problem.

The team tents foil over the unsauced meat for the final half of the cook to help break down fat and connective tissue. This avoids disturbing the bark with steam or boiling sauce in a tightly wrapped environment. The tenting approach came about accidentally from a moment of stubborn laziness. At a team gathering, a member put a bunch of shoulders on the pit for his church and then left them for the other members to deal with. Out of frustration, Lackie simply tented foil over the shoulders instead of wrapping them. The next day, his amazed teammate wanted to know how he achieved such a perfect bark.

Lackie first came to Memphis to attend the UT Medical School for dentistry. "It wasn't barbecue that I initially fell in love with. It was just food," he said. "I joined the team because my friends were on it, but I'm a research nerd." Lackie's experimentation with sauce got serious when he picked up a copy of Smoky Hale's *Great American Barbecue and Grilling Manuel* at a barbecue contest years ago. "I have no interest in copying a recipe. I'd rather look at twenty recipes and see what ingredients and ratios they have in common," Lackie said. "It's not about written down recipes. It's understanding how and why everything works. Memphis barbecue is based around a very balanced flavor—sweet, tart and spicy." Meanwhile, the team's shoulder and dry rub expert, Mark Lambert, was also honing his craft.

Lambert said that his rub is based around a flavor profile of salt, paprika, chili powder, onion, garlic, dried mustard, several kinds of ground pepper, celery salt and ginger. He also adds powdered versions of vinegar, tomato and Worcestershire. Getting the correct balance between salt and sugar is the most crucial part of the ratio, he said. "Competition barbecue is about coloring inside the lines," he added, referring to the need to stick to the traditional flavor profile. "The perfect balance of flavor is the goal."

Lambert and Lackie compared the products they were developing but didn't share their recipes with each other. "There was a point where both sides were just right," Lackie said. "It was not by either of us knowing the ingredients of the other. It was just knowing the flavor profile." The team began winning trophies at smaller circuit events around 1999 after holding an internal blind taste test of all the members' sauces. Lackie won out in that competition. His sauce ended up taking second place in the vinegar-based category at the 2000 Memphis in May competition. "You would've thought we'd won the whole thing," said Lackie, who still refers to that old recipe as his "mother sauce." "It was that trophy that really propelled us to really taking it seriously," he said. "We were all in our mid-twenties when we started this thing, and we were all just having fun. Sometimes we wouldn't even go to the awards ceremony."

Lackie believes that you "need to have a theme to your cooking process." While fruit juices like apple, orange and pineapple juice are common bastes for Memphis barbecue, he said that his team uses pureed apricot nectar. The idea came from experimenting with different fruit juice bastes and remembering the flavor of fried apricot pies that his mother made. He tried cooking three racks of ribs, with apple juice on one, pineapple on another and apricot on the third. The apricot ribs won his personal test with their flavor profile and gorgeous mahogany color. These days, the team mixes the nectar half and half with Sea God brewery's apricot beer for its baste. In keeping with his new flavor theme, Lackie began using apricot-infused white vinegar as the base for his sauce.

Great barbecue is an art. It is a product of knowledge, craftsmanship and vision. While restaurants cook in large quantities with an eye toward food cost and minimizing waste, competition cooks obsess over every detail of their food, carefully monitoring both the temperature of the pit and the internal temperature of the meat as they prepare small batches for judges to sample. Ironically, the barbecue from restaurants can be more satisfying than what takes home big trophies.

In the frantic push to create a perfect bite or two for a judge, competition teams sometimes go to extremes, like injecting meat or liberally seasoning it with sugar, margarine and MSG to get as much of a wow factor as possible.

But that intense flavor profile isn't necessarily something you want to make a meal out of. Cheap tricks like MSG and excessive sugar quickly wear out their welcome in a meal-sized portion.

Lackie said the trend toward "candy barbecue" seems worse in the KCBS circuit than in MBN. "In KCBS, the judges are really just trying a bite or two of each product," he said. "Since MBN also has the on-site judging, where we provide a good-sized serving, it forces people to scale back on the sugar since you don't want them walking away feeling like they're about to go into diabetic shock."

Lambert said the trick that bothers him the most is the growing trend of using curing rubs to produce an artificial smoke ring. A real smoke ring is produced by the nitrates in smoke curing meat. Curing rubs used on products like bacon and ham contain sodium nitrate along with seasonings like salt and sugar. That is where the pink color in ham comes from. Teams can coat meat with a curing rub and then wash it off after a few hours to produce the illusion of a smoke ring without the risk of creating too much dark, natural bark on the outside layer. While natural bark is the most delicious part of great barbecue, many judges are put off by the charred appearance. "Judges like an unnatural appearance, and an unnatural appearance is achieved with unnatural methods," Lambert said.

CHAPTER 11
CRAFTSMANSHIP

Creating barbecue for competition judges involves intense trial and error for even the most talented cooks. David Scott Walker was the executive chef at West 3rd Common in Manhattan when he returned to his hometown of Memphis in 2013 to escape the steady grind of the New York City restaurant world and spend time with his aging parents. "There's a much better pace of life down here," Walker said. While making plans to open his pork- and beer-centered German restaurant Schweinehaus in the revitalized Overton Square, a friend connected him with the Moody Ques Memphis in May team. After two meetings to discuss barbecue philosophy, the team brought him on as its head cook.

Walker's Schweinehaus restaurant represents another step forward for Overton Square, which was a hugely popular spot in the '70s but was mostly empty by the time Loeb Properties began buying up most of the property there with an ambitious plan to bring it back to life. "Overton Square died an unnatural death," said Loeb Properties president Bob Loeb, whose father founded the Loeb's Bar-B-Q chain during his Memphis real estate career. Colorado-based Fisher Capital Partners previously purchased most of the Square with plans to empty it and rebuild with a standard suburban-style design and mix of national chain businesses. Those plans met with loud disapproval from people in the Midtown community around the Square. "We always knew that if you just took what was there and fixed it up and leased it to local businesses, Memphians would come back," Loeb said.

Today, Overton Square is a vibrant mix of nightlife, local theater and retail. Walker hadn't chosen it as the location for the restaurant he was dreaming up when he took over the cooking responsibilities for the large, corporate-funded Moody Ques team, which operated out of a massive booth where serious barbecue traditionally took a backseat to nonstop partying. "We are in the transition from the party team to trying to build a foundation to win some trophies," Walker said. "From what I've heard in the past, even the cooks partied so much they would barely get food out to the team. It was just whiskey and beer and people passed out everywhere."

As the team's cook, Walker was responsible for providing breakfast, lunch and dinner to members, as well as cooking for the judges. "Last year was a huge learning experience. I got six hours' sleep in four days, and we finished middle of the pack." He had one helper during his first competition. For 2014, he is bringing his two sous chefs from his New York City restaurant days to assist him.

Walker is a graduate of the French Culinary Institute in Manhattan. A classic French background comes in handy around barbecue, since breaking down fat and connective tissue in tough cuts of meat with time and low temperature is a cornerstone of French technique. Wrapping barbecue in foil for the final part of a cook effectively re-creates the classic French technique of braising, where browned meats simmer in a closed pot while sitting in a small quantity of stock. In a foil wrap, the juices from the meat gather at the bottom while steam gathers at the top, creating the same conditions.

Experience in the competition circuit can provide a big advantage at Memphis in May. The Boar's Night Out team swept the MBN's Team of the Year honors for the circuit's highest point totals in ribs, shoulder and whole hog for both 2012 and 2013 with an eighteen-year-old pitmaster. Kendal Adair was in the sixth grade when he first competed in a youth contest in Southaven, Mississippi, where he came in second place. "I was hooked ever since," he said. "I've always loved to cook. When I was a little kid I wanted to watch the Emeril show on Saturday mornings instead of cartoons."

Adair will graduate from Olive Branch High School in the spring of 2014 and plans to get a community college degree in management and marketing before heading to culinary school to pursue his own restaurant dreams. His success with Boar's Night Out came from working with the team's longtime veterans like Allen Smith, who makes the rubs, and sauce cooks Bob Denton and Eric Hodson.

Memphis food and music are still evolving as new generations keep building on the past in innovative ways. The city has outstanding fine dining establishments—like Acre, Restaurant Iris and Andrew Michael

Italian Kitchen—where you won't see barbecue on the menu but where southern cooking still looms as a huge influence. Southern food evolved from the interaction of European, African and Native American people who borrowed the best ideas from each culture's culinary heritage hundreds of years before "fusion" became a culinary buzzword in the 1970s. The finest of European haute cuisine is rooted in the peasant-born French tradition of "waste nothing."

In many ways, it was a natural match, like when Howlin' Wolf and Muddy Waters first got their hands on electric guitars in the early 1940s, hot-wired them to the mono tube amps of AM-only radios in the dashboards of cars in small towns without home electricity and drew throngs of people to experience something that was entirely new yet totally organic in its development. Both the food and music of Memphis come from a culture of survival and speak to the elemental core of people throughout the globe.

As the decline of the Loeb's and Coleman's barbecue chains in the '70s laid the groundwork for a wide assortment of independent mom and pop restaurants, the implosion of the Memphis music industry in the same period led to a rich genre-spanning period of independent music. "Both Sun Studio and Stax had some of the same sort of do-it-yourself and do-it-the-way-you-want vibe. That mentality has always been in place," said Nan Hackman, who along with Memphian Robert Allen Parker co-directed the documentary *Meanwhile in Memphis: The Sound of a Revolution* about the city's post-Stax and post-Elvis explosion in underground music.

Stax's bankruptcy wasn't caused by a lack of demand for its music. "They got swept up in events that were way beyond their control," Hackman said. "A lot of industry people left town and went to Nashville, Los Angeles and New York, but the musicians stayed here and continued to make music even though there was no industry." She said that while making the documentary, now-deceased musician and music producer Jim Dickinson dismissed the industry suits, telling her, "They're not the talent. They don't understand it. They want to bring back the good old days but you can't build it from the top down."

Instead, the Memphis music scene rebuilt itself from the bottom up. "The underground is where the pulse and heartbeat was," Hackman said. The sound of Memphis soul and early rock helped shape the sound of later Memphis garage bands like Big Star, the Grifters and the Oblivians, along with early Memphis rappers like 8ball and MGJ. In the documentary, Grifters drummer David Shouse remarked, "Memphis is a good place for artists: It's cheap. Good food. People leave you alone, let you do your shit. Let you fuck up. Let you recover."

Rap DJs throughout the country relied on old Stax records for samples while listening to the sounds coming out of Memphis. "The Memphis rappers we talked to were all of one mind that everyone took from us," Hackman said. Meanwhile, the heavy touring by the Grifters and Oblivians greatly influenced musicians like Jack White during the later international garage rock revival.

Memphis music stores like Shangri La and Goner followed the Stax model of combining a music label with a retail store, which provided a valuable firsthand look at what customers were interested in. Goner Records is in Midtown's Cooper-Young neighborhood and hosts the annual Gonerfest that draws musicians and their fans from around the world to the dive bars of Memphis every September. "That was totally done through word of mouth and a website," Hackman said.

As Gonerfest has steadily grown throughout its decade-plus existence, it has also generated an international following for nearby Payne's Bar-B-Q. The Payne family learned to load the pit down in anticipation. "We always sell out," Candice Payne-Parker said. "The first year, the guys at Goner came and told us they were going to be sending people here, but we still weren't prepared for how many showed up. We get people from Dublin, Switzerland, Australia—all over the world—that week." The restaurant closes anywhere from 3:00 p.m. to 6:00 p.m. depending on how long the barbecue lasts. "When we're sold out, we're gone," Candice said.

Like in music, some of the best barbecue creations come from merging two old favorites to create something new, like the rib tip fried rice from KC's Southern Style Rice. KC's operates out of a bright-red trailer at a flea market at 4444 South 3rd Street, near Shelby Drive, Wednesdays through Saturdays. The rice is a creation of forty-seven-year-old Kirby Carter, who started working in the kitchen of a Whitehaven Chinese restaurant when he was fifteen years old. In 1996, Carter started offering a southern take on fried rice from his trailer-based kitchen. The still-available original options were smoked beef, chicken, ham, bologna, hamburger or a combination form with all those meats, whose smoke flavors permeate the rice and vegetables cooked in Carter's big commercial wok.

The rib tip fried rice followed a decade later, in about 2008, Carter said. All his meat is prepared in a giant barrel cooker behind his trailer, where he also offers foods like barbecue, burgers, catfish and smoked sausages. "I was just in there messing around one day. I had some rib tips and decided to throw them in." The result was an immediate hit with customers.

An order of rib tip fried rice comes with a side of barbecue sauce along with the traditional soy sauce and duck sauce. Because the rib tips include bone and cartilage, they are still a finger food, so the best way to experience the dish is with a fork in one hand eating the rice and vegetables, while using the other hand to dip rib tip pieces in the sauce and eat them. A large order is easily enough to feed two hungry people and still provide leftovers.

Rib tip fried rice first appeared around the same time that one of the oldest surviving name's in Memphis food and drink began wowing customers with a more traditional take on ribs. Alex's Tavern on Jackson Avenue in the Vollentine-Evergreen neighborhood is the oldest family-owned bar in Memphis. In a city known for partying late into the early-morning hours, it is a dive bar that pretty much never closes.

Opened in 1953 by Alex Kasaftes and currently owned and operated by his son, Rocky Kasaftes, the menu is incredibly short, but there isn't anything on it that isn't perfectly executed. It is a favorite after-work unwinding spot for restaurant and bar workers. While the late-night crowd enjoys burgers and wings, the ribs are generally reserved for the daytime patrons who come in to hang out and watch sports on the big-screen TVs.

Trying to heat up ribs late at night backs the grill up when people are clamoring for burgers, Rocky said. The ribs happened onto the menu in 2005 following one of the bar's annual Super Bowl parties where some of his friends cooked ribs for the feast. "I watched them and said, 'I can do this,'" he said.

It took him about six months of experimenting to perfect his surprisingly simple system. "You know when you get it. The people will let you know," he said. Decades before he thought about adding ribs to his menu, he received some business mentoring from one of the biggest names in ribs following the death of his father in 1978, when Rocky suddenly stepped into running the family business with his mother at the age of twenty-one.

"When daddy died, it was do or die," he said. When word of the family's struggles following the death of fifty-eight-year-old Alex reached Rendezvous founder Charles Vergos, he stopped by to offer Rocky some guidance. "When my daddy died, he came down here. The neighborhood was changing, and everybody wanted us to go out east. He said to me, 'Stay here. You make them come to you.' He shook my hand. He had a handshake that could drop you to your knees; he shook my hand and looked me in the eyes and said, 'You're Greek. You figure it out.'"

At the time, the restaurant served ham sandwiches and burgers. Rocky jokes that he likes to make little changes to the menu "every fifteen years or so." His mom, Eugenia, made the burger patties by hand at her home, where she also did the bookkeeping, while Rocky handled the day-to-day operations of the tavern. Eugenia passed away in 2011 at the age of seventy-nine.

"I miss both my parents," Rocky said. "Both of them were just good, hardworking people. They were both characters; a Greek and an Irish woman." The restaurant's method of steaming its famous Greek burgers under Eugenia's old cake pan top came from Alex, who was fond of steaming steaks under the same top at home while Rocky was growing up. The problem was that he would often decide to use it late at night after work and then put it back on a delicate, freshly baked cake without washing it. "I'd wake up to her shouting, 'You ruined my cake!'"

The Greek seasoning used on the burgers is also an integral element of the ribs. When questioned about it, a bartender joked, "Everything here is seasoned with it. If you sit still long enough, we're liable to sprinkle some on you." Rocky rubs the ribs down with a simple mix of Greek seasoning and black pepper and cooks them by the case over pans full of apple juice on a Tucker Cooker with a side-mounted firebox. Rocky insists on shopping locally to stock his kitchen. The ribs come from Charlie's Meat Market on Summer, while the ground beef for his burgers comes from the High Point Grocery. He doesn't bother making his own beans and slaw since there is already a Tops Bar-B-Q half a block from his tavern. He simply buys both from there and hits them with Greek seasoning before serving them.

He cooks the ribs for eight hours at about 225 degrees, basting them with apple juice throughout the process. After six or seven hours, he gives them a final baste before wrapping them in foil. After a couple more hours in the Tucker, he piles them into a cooler for them to steep. Before serving the ribs, he quickly dips them in the same sauce he uses for his Greek wings—a simple 3:1 mix of Wicker's and Lea & Perrins Worcestershire sauce. The sauce he serves on the side is simply store-bought Rendezvous sauce spiced up with the ubiquitous Greek seasoning.

He uses a mix of water-soaked apple and hickory wood with charcoal briquettes in the firebox. And he tosses in an onion and a pack of bacon when he starts the fire. If there isn't any bacon handy, he tosses in a couple hamburger patties instead. "Any book you read says don't ever throw fat in a fire, but it gets the whole neighborhood smelling good," he said.

The Tucker Cooker Rocky uses is owned by J.C. Youngblood, who works at the downtown location of Central BBQ. Youngblood played softball with Rocky and would tease him about the state of the old barrel cooker he originally used that was propped up with bricks and lined with tinfoil.

"Rocky is kind of like my adopted uncle," Youngblood laughed. "I loaned it to him, but whenever I get it and use it, he bugs me about, 'When am I going to have it back? When am I going to have it back?' He bugs me about my cooker."

The Central BBQ where Youngblood works is around the corner from where the Tucker Cookers are manufactured. Its inventor, George Karcher, didn't set out to go into the cooker business. His company, Tri-State Bodyworks on Carolina Avenue, built custom truck bodies dating back to the 1940s, when it was founded by Albert Tucker. "I grew up in this shop," said Karcher, whose dad, Oliver Karcher, bought the company in the '60s.

As the owner of a metal fabrication business a few blocks south of Tom Lee Park, where the annual Memphis in May barbecue contest is held, Karcher was frequently asked to work on people's barbecue cookers. In fact, he said that he figured out how to make the pellet feeder work on John Willingham's W'ham Turbo Cooker when Willingham adapted his rotisserie cooker from charcoal and wood to hardwood pellets in the late '80s. He also helped refine it into something that could be mass-produced instead of requiring custom fabrication. "I kind of cleaned it up," Karcher said. "I looked at it from a manufacturing point. He looked at it from a barbecue perspective."

Karcher began daydreaming his own vision of a perfect cooker. "You put it together a million times in your head," he said. "One day, I told my wife, 'I'm going to go out here and build this thing I have in my head.' I wanted a cooker that I could smoke a whole hog with, but I like steaks and hamburgers as much as I like barbecue, so I wanted to be able to use it as a grill too."

His design has a main cooking chamber with a charcoal tray that can be raised for direct grilling or lowered for above-heat barbecue. And it has a side firebox for completely indirect heat. Everything comes apart to make the entire contraption easy to hose out. The first completed cooker was sitting in his shop when Mike Simpson of Quality Stoves on South 3rd, who also helped redesign Willingham's Turbo Cooker, saw it and immediately told Karcher that he wanted to buy fifteen of them.

While technological bells and whistles can be impressive, there is an inherent beauty to any design that is rugged, simple and utterly reliable. "It just works," Karcher said. In a world where a growing number of barbecue cookers are rotisserie contraptions that are either gas-assisted or pellet-fed, the Tucker is a simple device that is sturdy, easy to clean and, most importantly, will hold a steady 225-degree temperature for hours using surprisingly little fuel.

Any hood or firebox from any Tucker Cooker will fit any other Tucker, which allows Karcher to keep replacement parts in stock for any customer who manages to break one of them. But breaking something takes effort. "The body of this thing is made of the same steel we made dump truck bodies from," Karcher said.

While he has to steadily adjust his prices with the price of steel, in early 2014, the base price for a Tucker Cooker was $3,695. The total price approached $6,000 with enough additional options like chrome and stainless steel parts, as well as an additional food warmer for above the firebox.

"Nothing leaves here that isn't perfect. I've never had anybody bring one back. I've never had anybody call with a problem," Karcher said. He focuses on quality over quantity. He built the first cooker in 2004, and ten years later, he was getting number 1,585 ready for its new owner. The cookers are well represented each year at the Memphis in May contest down the hill from his shop, used by numerous teams. Karcher has entered his own team several years just to set up cookers for any customers who want to experience the event firsthand without the expense of forming their own team and bringing their own gear.

The success of the cookers, combined with increasingly strict Department of Transportation rules that created constant regulation headaches for his truck business, led Karcher to abandon vehicles to focus on the cookers. "I did not have this vision in my head," he said while motioning to the Tucker Cooker plant that has overtaken his old business.

The world of Memphis barbecue is crowded with talented pitmasters hawking their products anywhere they can. Richard Forrest, an alumni from the Cozy Corner's pit, sells barbecue from an outdoor barrel cooker around the corner from it in front of the Hi-Tone on Cleveland in the Crosstown neighborhood. The Midtown music venue relocated to Cleveland Street in 2013 after operating for fifteen years out of the Poplar Avenue building that once housed the karate dojo where Elvis Presley trained under Master Kang Rhee.

The new Hi-Tone is across the street from the towering, Art Deco 1.4-million-square-foot Crosstown Sears building, which was constructed in 1927 as a combination retail store and distribution center for the Sears catalogue during a period when it was a defining force for American consumers. Sears closed the facility in 1989, and it sat rotting and abandoned before renovation work began in 2014 to turn it into a mixed-use center for medical offices, apartments and retail.

Richard Forrest's outdoor cooking rig serves as the kitchen for the new Hi-Tone. He contacted owner Jonathan Kiersky about selling barbecue at the original venue's closing in February 2013. Kiersky told him to stay in touch because he was planning to find a new home for the club. The thirty-eight-year-old Forrest began working at the Cozy Corner at the age of sixteen when Raymond Robinson was still alive and manning the pit.

"He showed me some things, but I wasn't able to get on the pit then because I was too young, so I just watched," Forrest said. Following Robinson's death, Forrest ended up working the pit for ten years, but he dreamed of working for himself. His grandfather Franklin Jones was known for barbecue in Mumford, Tennessee, where he operated a stand in his front yard. "It's in my blood to barbecue," Forrest said.

He lives in the neighborhood where he grew up, near the Cozy Corner and Hi-Tone, witnessing the area's recent revitalization and hoping to have his own restaurant there one day. Until then, he has a loyal following among the music fans who frequent the Hi-Tone at night.

While most restaurant pitmasters wait for customers to come to them, Eddie "Boss Man" Patterson takes his pit to the people. The fifty-year-old Patterson owns the Boss Man Pit Stop in a former Loeb's Bar-B-Q location on Getwell just north of I-240. But the majority of his business comes from the food truck he takes to Memphis-area clubs late at night and into the early hours of the morning.

He was cooking at the restaurant back when it was a barbecue joint called Chuck's, which later resurfaced as Papa Chuck's on Airways. "I've always loved to cook," Patterson said. He refurbished houses after the Chuck's owner closed the restaurant to focus on catering. But he still had the cooking bug and ended up with an old boiler discarded by the Paramount Uniform building. "It looked like a grill. It had the legs on it and the frame around it," he said. With a little modification, he had a barbecue cooker that he started pulling behind a trailer.

Meanwhile, several non-barbecue restaurants moved into the old building on Getwell, but none of them lasted long before Patterson moved in around 2008 and brought the old pit back to life. "It gives the best flavor to me," he said. "A lot of people are going to the gas pits now. I don't like that. I like my meat smoked. People will try to cook with gas and just put liquid smoke in their sauce."

When he moved into the restaurant, he didn't stop hitting the club circuit. He posts on Instagram with the handle bossman901 to let customers know where to find him. "When I pull up, they're already there. Rain, sleet or snow, we go," he said. "A lot of club owners hit me up on Instagram because wherever the Bossman is at, that's where the people are going to go." On nights he runs the truck, he frequently sells food until 4:30 or 5:00 a.m. and then returns to the restaurant to get its pit fired up around 6:00 a.m. in order to open at 11:00 a.m., while stealing a few hours of sleep in the back of the building.

"It's hard out there doing what I do," Patterson said. "You got a lot of haters out there, whatever you do. They'll do anything to slow you down." One of his biggest setbacks came when someone stole the barbecue cooker and trailer he was pulling with an RV. He bounced back by buying a used box truck from Brim's Snack Foods, which is known throughout the Mid-South for its potato chips, pork rinds and cheese puffs. He paid $5,000 to have someone remove the rear lift hatch and re-create the charcoal pit from his restaurant in the back of the truck.

Along with pork, beef brisket and chicken, Patterson cooks barbecue lamb, which is commonly found in Kentucky. His version is incredibly tender and served with his mustard-heavy barbecue sauce. A friend of his encountered it while out of town and asked Patterson to attempt it. His rendition became a permanent menu item.

Patterson makes his own sauce and rub at the restaurant. The rub has a nice chili powder and pepper kick that goes great with the mustardy sauce. "It's good on everything," he said. He uses Boston butts for his chopped pork, stating that while shoulders are cheaper per pound, too much of that weight comes from skin, fat and bone. "You go through all that and say, 'I should have just got me a butt.'"

His devotion to his patrons has earned Patterson some big-name customers in the Memphis community. The lamb was a request from a member of rapper Yo Gotti's entourage. Patterson is usually outside any Memphis venue where Gotti or any of the other rappers on his CMG roster are performing. Patterson said that CMG artists frequently send for food from the truck, and during the day, Gotti will send people from his Southwind home to pick up carryout orders. Other fans include Grizzlies players like Zach Randolph, who loves the barbecue nachos, and Tony Allen, who has a seemingly endless appetite for the burgers. "He gets a sack full of them," said Patterson's wife, Patricia Patterson.

"When I was young, I used to think people on TV were unreachable until my husband had a dream to open a restaurant," said Patricia, who is usually at her husband's side both in the truck and the restaurant. "You really get to see how down-to-earth some people are."

Like artists in other mediums, the people who work in barbecue get creative about finding outlets for their craft. "You've got to have a passion for this. You got to love it," said Ray Nolan. The sixty-year-old self-professed Dr. Barbecue operates out of an old ambulance bus that normally sits on the side of Elvis Presley Boulevard just north of Brook Road, unless Nolan has it at an event like an Ole Miss football game. He said that he has owned thirteen different restaurants in places like Greenville, Mississippi; Covington, Tennessee; Ripley, Tennessee; and Boonesville, Mississippi, over the past thirty-eight years. "I've been all around."

He picked up the bus a little over a year ago but has had the massive buggy-sprung cooker he pulls behind it for eighteen years. "I pull that around because it gets a lot of attention," he said. Nolan wants to create a commercial version of his sauce to sell in stores.

His shoulder meat gets its impressive smoke flavor and bark from the mix of charcoal and woods like cherry, pecan and hickory that he burns in his pit. Nolan said that he picked up the bus for $1,500; "$900,000 is what this thing cost the taxpayers," he said. It still includes an assortment of old cabinets and medical equipment. He warms up food underneath an Infant Warming System for newborns.

The bus in its original form was the brainchild of Dr. Sheldon B. Korones, who worked at the newborn center at the Regional Medical Center at Memphis, according to registered nurse Betty Loughridge, who has been with the Med since 1978. The Med is the Mid-South's premier trauma center, with a highly renowned neonatal Intensive Care Unit (ICU). Korones founded the hospital's newborn center, which is now named after him, in 1968 and quickly recognized the need for a dedicated transport system for infants.

The first in 1979 was a converted bread truck, Loughridge said. It covered a five-hundred-mile area around Memphis through Tennessee, Mississippi and Arkansas. In the early '80s, it was replaced by a Winnebago. "We would get a call from an outlying hospital that had an emergency they weren't equipped to handle," she said. "They would call us, and our doctors would tell their doctors what to do until we could get there." The mobile infant centers always traveled with a doctor and nurse on board, with a fireman driving.

"It had everything we had in our unit," Loughridge said. "[Korones] didn't want any baby to not survive because they couldn't get to a hospital. His goal was that every child had the right to live." The Med sold the bus in 2005, the same year Korones retired. "There were times when we'd be broke down on the side of the road, and it was costing us more to keep it running." By then, the Med had partnered with nearby Le Bonheur Hospital to use

Ray Nolan, who bills himself as "Dr. Barbecue," operates out of a former ambulance bus that once cared for infants on their way to the Regional Medical Center at Memphis. The bus still contains a lot of its old medical equipment, like the infant warming station behind Nolan to the left.

its modern infant-dedicated ambulances. Korones passed away in 2013 at the age of eighty-nine, but his work at the newborn center is credited with saving the lives of fifty thousand premature babies.

Many competition pitmasters have dreams of owning their own restaurants. Ty's Smokehouse Bar-B-Q opened in the former Wolfchase-area location of A&R Bar-B-Q in 2013. Owner Ty Theisen began competing in the KCBS circuit eight years earlier with his team, the TNT Smokers. While he has helped friends with Memphis in May teams, he has never entered his team there. But his passion for competition barbecue is still evident in his restaurant.

"This is something I've always wanted to do," he said. "It's always kind of been on the back of my mind." The fifty-five-year-old Iowa transplant first moved to Memphis thirty years ago to build hotels. He immediately fell in love with the food. "You can't be in Memphis twenty minutes without smelling barbecue," he said. He decided that he couldn't wait for retirement to pursue his own barbecue dream. "I decided, 'If I wait another five years I won't have the energy to do it.' You have to go for that dream when it gets in your head," he said. The roughly chopped, mustardy slaw at Ty's includes a dusting of dry rub mixed in with it. The ribs have a nice bark, well-rendered fat and good smoke penetration that makes them good enough to enjoy without sauce.

Shortly after Ty's opened, another competition-inspired barbecue restaurant popped up just north of Memphis in Atoka, Tennessee, on Highway 51, when the former Post Office Bar-B-Que building reopened as the Paradise Grill. Post Office cooked outstanding pulled pork with an incredibly deep smoke ring, but like many great barbecue cooks, the owner had troubles with the business side of the operation.

Paradise owner Mike Godwin started competing in the MBN circuit with his Paradise Porkers team in 2009. The forty-six-year-old said that he started the team after trying some of the barbecue that other people were cooking at Memphis in May. "Me and a buddy were standing on top of one of the rigs down there, and he said, 'You know, your ribs are better than these.'" Godwin first entered the Memphis in May competition in 2011.

He owned the Daily Grind deli and coffee shop in downtown Memphis from 2000 to 2005 while also working for FedEx. When he retired from FedEx after twenty-five years, he decided to jump back into the restaurant business. "I never thought I'd do it in Atoka," he laughed. "I thought I'd do it in Florida."

When Post Office Bar-B-Que closed, the owner took his cooker with him. So, when Godwin moved into the building, he set up the same Cadillac Cooker he uses in competition behind it. He is having a gas-fired pit constructed since the rigors of daily restaurant cooking are quickly wearing away the competition cooker's burn box. Maintaining a 250-degree temperature inside the cooker, which uses a rotisserie so the meats baste one another with fat drippings as they rotate, requires a 1,400-degree temperature in the box of burning lump charcoal and cherry wood. Godwin said that he will continue using the combination in the gas-fired cooker when he switches over. He waits to split the cherry wood until right before it goes in the burn box to maintain as much of its flavor and aroma as possible.

"I started with hickory and wasn't winning anything. I switched to fruitwood and started winning," Godwin explained. "We do everything to the specs of our competition meat. It's all the same as we serve in competition." Like Rocky Kasaftes at Alex's Tavern, Godwin wraps his meat in foil toward the end of a cook, and after it is pulled from the cooker, he places it in large coolers to steep in the foil. "The secret to any barbecue is continuous heat," he said.

While plenty of Memphis-area barbecue restaurateurs have competition trophies on display, no one else has a collection equal to the one at Memphis Barbecue Company on Goodman Road in the Memphis suburb of Horn Lake, Mississippi. The restaurant is a partnership between Pete and Melissa Cookston of the Yazoo Delta Q team and John Wheeler of the Natural Born Grillers team. Wheeler's awards include first-place Memphis in May trophies for ribs from 2010 and 2012 and for whole hog combined with the grand championship from 2008. Meanwhile, the Cookstons won first place in whole hog each year from 2010 through 2012, with grand championships in 2010 and 2012. To top it off, the couple also won the grand championship at the inaugural Kingsford Invitational Competition in 2012.

The invitational competition, hosted by the Kingsford charcoal company, features the winners of every major barbecue competition throughout the country from every circuit, Pete Cookston said. He began cooking barbecue in college, and when he and Melissa married sixteen years ago, one of the first things they did together was enter a barbecue contest. They only entered a few a year due to the cost of competing, but as their skills improved, they began paying attention to the hefty prize purses awarded to top teams. "We had done decent, and in 2007, we said, 'We can win these things,'" Pete said. The competition circuit became a full-time job for them, which could be perilously feast or famine. "You lose, and you're going to be eating tuna fish for a few weeks."

The Cookstons had decades of combined experience in regional restaurant management, so following two years of big-time Memphis in May success, they partnered with Wheeler to open Memphis Barbecue Company in December 2011. The restaurant was an immediate hit. Despite its location flanked by national chains like Applebee's and Cracker Barrel in an overdeveloped suburban commercial center off Goodman Road next to I-55, it represents an oasis of quality and service in a desert of corporate mediocrity.

The delicious aroma of barbecue envelopes the parking lot thanks to an industrial-sized Ole Hickory cooker loaded exclusively with pecan. Instead of the dinner rolls common at most restaurants, meals start with baskets of fresh-made pork rinds dusted with dry rub. The Memphis Barbecue Company offers both loin (baby back) and St. Louis–cut spare ribs. The fresh pork rinds are also available on a concoction called the "crunch burger," a gloriously big, sloppy double cheeseburger topped with a giant pork rind. The restaurant has a great spicy barbecue sauce along with a sweet, mild version, but both varieties of ribs are good enough to enjoy with just the light dusting of rub that comes on them when ordered dry. The rub and rendered fat create their own sauce as they mingle together.

The company has expanded, with new locations in North Carolina and Georgia. All the restaurants are company-owned, new managers have to travel to the Horn Lake location for training and Pete and Melissa Cookston regularly visit the other locations. Everything is made from scratch in the restaurants' kitchens, and employees are trained to toss food that doesn't measure up to the owners' standards.

Maintaining competition-level quality is a constant challenge welcomed by owners who compete in whole hog. "It's our favorite because it's the most challenging," Pete said of the category. A team can cook a lot of ribs to select perfect samples for judging, but with whole hog, that kind of hedging isn't possible. The restaurant doesn't use whole hogs since there would be too much waste to make it practical. But the necessary attention to detail carries over.

CHAPTER 12
HUSTLE

The level of competition in the world of Memphis barbecue makes success a struggle. When Pollard's Bar-B-Q moved from a location near Airways and Shelby Drive it had called home for fifteen years to a bigger building just south of Graceland on Elvis Presley Boulevard in 2011, it lost longtime customers who didn't know where it had gone, according to owner Tarrance Pollard.

Pollard was simultaneously struggling with expenses from the move. One of the biggest expenses came from his decision to relocate his brick-and-steel barbecue pit to the new building, which already had a pit since it had been home to Arnold's Bar-B-Q before that restaurant moved farther east into the suburbs on Shelby Drive. The old Arnold's pit had vent problems and would fill the building with smoke. Pollard decided that he would rather shoulder the expense of relocating his familiar old pit rather than attempt to straighten out an unfamiliar, cantankerous one someone else had already decided to abandon.

A little over a year after the move, the restaurant's struggles landed it on the cable TV show *Restaurant: Impossible* in an episode that originally aired in late May 2012. The show's premise is that celebrity chef Robert Irvine visits troubled restaurants and spends two days and $10,000 trying to turn things around.

Pollard grew up around barbecue. His grandfather, Alonzo Pollard Jr., had a barbecue pit at his house before his death in 1985 at the age of sixty-eight. "He taught everybody how to barbecue," Tarrance said. Tarrance's uncle founded A&R Bar-B-Q, and his father, Alonzo III, makes the homemade hot link sausages sold at Pollard's and A&R. The forty-eight-year-old Tarrance worked for A&R for eight years starting in the mid-'80s before opening his own restaurant.

The *Restaurant: Impossible* crew heavily renovated the restaurant's Spartan interior, which fits with conventional thinking about improving a restaurant. But a Memphis-area barbecue joint isn't a typical restaurant. Places like Payne's, Alex's and the Cozy Corner have made it abundantly clear that Memphians will readily venture into the most well worn of dives as long as they know they can count on great barbecue and friendly service.

Beyond the publicity, the best thing Pollard's got out of *Restaurant: Impossible* was Irvine's advice to pare down the menu and make as much food as possible from scratch. Irvine stressed how much Tarrance could slash food costs by making sides from scratch. The resulting fresh-made baked beans and French fries are also much better than standard packaged fare.

While Pollard's needed to make some changes, like all "reality" shows, *Restaurant: Impossible* spent a lot of time intentionally creating needless tension so the episode could have drama. The TV show used a self-imposed two-day deadline to completely renovate the entire restaurant—thrashing to redo the building's wiring while customers lined up outside for a grand reopening.

When Irvine tried to show Tarrance the "right way" to season ribs, he did it with an Asian-inspired recipe full of ginger and soy sauce. For a barbecue restaurant near Graceland to be successful, it needs to serve food with a distinctly Memphis flavor, not something that would be seen as an interesting take on barbecue to serve in Atlantic City. One of the wonderful things about eating barbecue is that there is no single right way to do it. But to be successful in Memphis, your best bet is to stick to the traditional flavor profile. Tarrance did change his sauce recipe, but he still went with a Memphis-style mix of tomato, vinegar, sugar and spice.

The episode gave Pollard's national exposure. Out-of-state license plates are now common in the parking lot. "People come to visit Graceland, and they saw us on TV so they come on down," Tarrance said. And he has seen an increase in local customers thanks to the show, which has helped stabilize the business. He can tell any time the episode gets rerun by the bump in business.

There are two other barbecue restaurants along Elvis Presley Boulevard in the mile and a half of road between Pollard's and Graceland. One of them, Big Bill Bar-B-Que, is owned by a man who was once married into the Pollard family and employed at A&R. The other, Marlowe's Ribs, has been around since the '70s and is known for the fleet of pink limousines it uses to bring customers to and from Graceland-area hotels free of charge. But despite the competition, Tarrance has a passion for the family trade. "It's a tough job, but I'd rather be doing this than anything else," he said.

Running a successful barbecue joint can represent the ultimate dream even for Memphians who have achieved stardom in other arts. While discussing his plans for the future during a February 28, 2014 interview with the *Commercial Appeal*, Paul Beauregard, who cofounded the rap group Three 6 Mafia as DJ Paul, said, "One day, I'm going to have my own barbecue joint. That's the plan." Beauregard already sells his DJ Paul–branded sauce and rub online and in stores. It's a labor of love for a thirty-seven-year-old who has already toured the world, won an Oscar for his work on the *Hustle & Flow* soundtrack and sold more than 20 million albums.

But Memphis is also a place where anyone with a barrel cooker and confidence in their dream can try to hustle their way to success. Someone with a good eye can find great barbecue hiding along the road just by knowing some of the signs. The Macon Country Store at the rural three-way intersection of Highway 193, Macon Drive and Oakland Road in nearby Fayette County is an easy-to-overlook building that demonstrates some of the key indicators of good rural barbecue. It's a "country store," which usually means that some sort of southern plate lunches are offered. It has a large barrel cooker in front of it with a firebox separate from the main cooking chamber, which means barbecue. Finally, there is a large woodpile behind the store, indicating real, old-fashioned technique.

Husband and wife owners Emmet and Cathy Kimble purchased the Macon Country Store in 2011. Emmet worked as a maintenance contractor in the restaurant industry for thirty-five years before arthritis made working with tools too difficult. "I was suffering a lot out there, and my wife and I weren't seeing near enough of each other," he said. "This gave us our time together."

On the counter of the store, there is a handwritten one-page book entitled *How to Clean Your Smokers and Grills for Dummies*. It's a short work that reads, "1. Make sure your fire is out! 2. Make sure your fire is out! 3. See first two!" Emmet, who grew up in a large family deep in the Delta in Greenville, Mississippi, explained that he cleans the cooker by using a large quantity of lighter fluid to burn out all the accumulated grease. In 2013, he tried to clean it unaware that there were still embers in the firebox. The fluid drained down into the firebox, creating a blast that knocked him twelve feet through the air. He is proud of his new eyebrows, which finally grew back in after about a year. "My nickname is now Flash Boomer. It burnt me pretty good," he said.

Even inside the Memphis city limits, barrel cookers and great barbecue can hide off the road at places like Elwood's Shack, a little building tucked away in the parking lot of a Lowe's hardware store at Summer and Graham. One of the owner's, Tim Bednarski, is from Texas, and Elwood's offers great brisket sandwiches alongside the standard Memphis-style pork. After opening in early 2013, the hard-to-spot restaurant has already built a loyal following. And farther out in the suburbs on Macon, just a few miles from the Morris Grocery, the Pork Choppers competition team opened a barbecue restaurant in early 2014 called PC BBQ inside a Golf Center, cooking with portable barrel cookers in the parking lot.

It is impossible to create a definitive guide to Memphis barbecue because the landscape is constantly evolving. Memphis has suffered numerous tragedies and setbacks, but surviving them has shaped its culture. Singing about their hometown on their song "One More Last Goodbye," locally based roots country band the Dead Soldiers intone, "She's just a bird with a broken wing / but man you should hear her sing / a song so sad and sweet it'll make you cry." The city is known for soul music and soul food. The recurring use of that word is no coincidence. "Soul" implies an inner spirit, a true essence, something real and honest. Something that embodies all the pain, wisdom, suffering, joy and individual expression that make life the grand experience it is.

INDEX

A

Abe's Bar-B-Q 20
Adair, Kendal 105
Alex's Tavern 108–110, 116, 120
A&R Bar-B-Q 73, 120

B

barbecue nachos 67
barbecue pizza 25
barbecue spaghetti 48
Bar-B-Q Shop 47–50, 52, 77
bark 17, 64, 101, 103
Barlow, William 19, 26, 45
Barnes, George "Machine Gun Kelly" 23
BBQ Joints: Stories and Secret Recipes from the Barbeque Belt 20
Beale Street
  and E.H. Crump 26
  barbecue 65–67
  decline 30, 33
  nineteenth century 19
  red-light district 19
  revitalization 61, 65–67

Beale Street: Resurrection of the Home of the Blues 19, 33, 61
Beauregard, Paul 121
Blondis, Craig 90–93
Boar's Night Out 105
Boss Man Pit Stop 112
Boston butt 13, 21, 29, 72, 85, 95, 113
Bozo's Hot Pit Bar-B-Q 20
Bradley, Bobby 55
Brady and Lil's 47–50, 53, 77
Briggs, Damon 73
Brown, Dan 43, 75
Brownsville, Tennessee 69

C

Canale's Grocery 11
Captain John's 12, 36
Carter, Kirby 107
Cave's Soul Food and More 50
Central BBQ 59, 90–93, 109, 110
Cerrito, Michael 88
Charcoal Store 57–59, 66, 67
cocaine 19
Coleman, A.B. 36, 39

Coleman's Bar-B-Q 36, 39, 40, 45, 106
cole slaw 21, 55
Coletta's 25
Coley, Dr. Bill 79
Compton, James 53
Conaway, Dan 46
Cookston, Pete and Melissa 117
Corky's Bar-B-Q 51, 52, 94–97
Cozy Corner 54–56
Crosstown Neighborhood Association
    62
Crump, E.H. 26
Culpepper's Chicken Shack 47

D

Dalton, Mark 72
Dead Soldiers (band) 122
De Soto, Hernando 18
Dickinson, Jim 106
DJ Paul 121
Double J Smokehouse 59, 93
"Dr. Barbecue" (Ray Nolan) 114
drive-in 21
dry rub 32, 64, 76, 84, 101

E

Elkington, John 19, 33, 47, 61, 65
Elwood's Shack 122

F

Fat Head 14
Fat Larry's 81
Forrest, Richard 111
Fortune's Jungle Garden 21
Franklin, Dale 27, 30

G

Gallagher, Neil 99
Gelin, David 20
Germantown Commissary 67, 77
Godwin, Mike 116
Gonerfest 107
Gordon, Robert 46

Graceland 43, 47, 74, 75, 119, 120
Green, Laurie B. 26
Gridley, Clyde 50, 78
Gridley's Bar-B-Q 50, 53, 78

H

Hackman, Nan 106
Hale, Smoky 101
Harkins, John E. 46
Helen's Bar-B-Q 69
Heuberger, Leonard 20, 43, 49, 76
Hi-Tone 111
Hobson, Lynn 60
Hog Wild Catering 68
Howlin' Wolf (Chester Arthur Burnett)
    28, 30, 106
Hughes, Bill 20, 21, 23, 44, 48
Hughes, Thelma 23
Hughes, Tommy Leonard 44

I

Interstate Bar-B-Q 49, 52, 54, 94–96
Itayem, Adam 83–85
Ivy, Jack 78

J

Jack's Bar-B-Q Rib Shack 11, 48, 59,
    79–81
Jackson, Tennessee 71
Johnson, Carl 50
Johnson, Joe Lee 52
Johnson, Robert 20
Johnston, Robert 81
*John Willingham's World Champion Bar-
    B-Q* 21, 64
Justine's 39, 46, 74

K

Kansas City Barbeque Society (KCBS)
    80, 88, 89, 103
Karcher, George 110
Kasaftes, Alex 108
Kasaftes, Rocky 108–110, 116

KC's Southern Style Rice 107
Keith, Lierre 17
Kiersky, Jonathan 111
Kimble, Cathy and Emmet 121
King, B.B. 28, 30
King, Dr. Martin Luther, Jr. 45, 46
KWEM radio 27, 28, 30

L

Lackie, Dr. Richard 99–103
Lambert, Mark 101–103
Lamm, Preston 65
Latham, Paul 71
Latham's Meat Company 71
Leonard's Pit Barbecue 20, 43, 49, 52,
      75, 79
Loeb, Bob 46, 50, 104
Loeb, Henry 36, 46
Loeb Properties 104
Loeb's Bar-B-Q 36, 38–40, 45, 46, 50,
      59, 60, 80, 82, 106, 112
   logo 60, 83, 84
Loeb, William 36, 39, 40, 46
*Looking Up at Down: The Emergence of
      Blues Culture* 19, 26, 45
Loughridge, Betty 114

M

Macon Country Store 121
Marcum, Blake 99
Maxwell, William 28
Mayes, Larry 80
McAfee, Brent 64
McClendon, Helen 60, 82
McFalls, Richard 36, 47
*Meanwhile in Memphis: The Sound of a
      Revolution* 106
Mellor, Ernie 68
Memphis Barbecue Company 117
Memphis Barbecue Network (MBN)
      80, 88, 89, 99, 103, 105
"Memphis Barbecue Restaurant Ghost
      Pit Chronicles" blog (Richard
      McFalls) 36, 47

*Memphis Chronicles: Bits of History from the
      Best Times* 46
Memphis in May
   2013 barbecue competition 98–105
   and deaths of Donald Pelts and John
      Willingham 97
   barbecue contest begins 61
   growth of 86–89
   success of Memphis Barbecue Com-
      pany owners at contest 117
Montague, George 42
Moody Ques 104
Morris Grocery 56
Moss, Porter 36, 40
Moye, Robert 52

N

Natural Born Grillers 117
Naughton, Tom 14
Neely, Barbara 53
Neely, Jim 49, 52–54, 94
Neely, Pat and Gina 94
Nolan, Ray 114

O

Ogle, Jimmy 46, 61, 66, 86
Orpheum Theatre 61
Overton Square
   Public Eye 51
   revitalization 104
   Schweinehaus 104
   Silky O'Sullivan's 86

P

Paradise Grill 116
Patterson, Eddie and Patricia 112
Payne family (Emily, Flora, Horton and
      Ronald) 57
Payne-Parker, Candice 57, 107
Payne's Bar-B-Q 56, 107
PC BBQ 122
Peabody Hotel 30, 33, 35, 50, 67
Pelts, Barry and Donald 51, 97
Picasso, Pablo 17

Pig-N-Whistle 23, 77, 91
Pollard family (Alonzo Jr., Alonzo III,
    Andrew, Brian and Tarrance)
    73, 119
Pollard's Bar-B-Q 119–121
Pork Choppers 122
Pork University 87
Presley, Elvis
    Coletta's Pizza 25
    death 47
    karate dojo 111
    Leonard's Pit Barbecue 43
    on Beale Street 27
    on KWEM and at Sun Studio 30
    part of Bellevue renamed for him 75
prohibition 19, 26
Public Eye 51

R

Ray, James Earl 46
Redding, Otis 45
Reisling, Bob 62
Rendezvous 32–36, 47, 64, 67, 108
René, Wendy 45
rib tip fried rice 107
Richey, Joe 23
Robertson, Charlie 60, 81–83
Robinson, Raymond 55, 112
Rudolph, James 87
Rum Boogie Café 65
Rupert, Bill 23, 77

S

Sapps, Roger 90–93
Schweinehaus 104
shoulder 13, 21, 29, 52, 60, 63, 72, 85,
    95, 113
Shouse, David 106
Showboat Barbecue 36, 40
Simpson, Mike 98, 110
smoke ring 18, 103
Southern Foodways Alliance 35, 42, 70
Southern Soul-Blues 30
Stax 45–47, 65, 106, 107

St. Jude Children's Research Hospital
    55
Sturgius, Tom 83
Sugliano, Edith 49
Sullivan, Thomas "Silky" 86
Sun Studio 30, 106
Sweet Swine O' Mine 99–103

T

Taylor, Walker 67
Thomas, Marvell 46, 47
Three 6 Mafia 121
Three Little Pigs 11, 36, 48, 59, 81
Tom's Bar-B-Q and Deli 83–85
Too Sauced to Pork 99
Tops Bar-B-Q 36, 41, 63
Trailer Pork 88
Tucker Cooker 109, 110
Turner, Helen 69–71
Ty's Smokehouse Bar-B-Q 115

U

urban renewal 33, 46

V

Vegetarian Myth 17
Vergos, Charles 32–35, 108
Vergos, John 35
Vernon family (Eric, Frank and Hazel)
    47–49, 77
Vieron, Reverend Nicholas L. 35
Vincent, Brady 47–49, 53

W

Walker, David Scott 104
Walker, Doug and Jamie 79
WDIA radio 30
West Memphis, Arkansas 27, 28, 30
Wheeler, John 117
Whitaker family (Jack, Jack Jr., Jack III,
    Joe and Sharon) 59, 79–81
Whitehead, Vernon "Pert" 57, 58, 59,
    66

Whiteis, David 30
William's Bar-B-Q 28
Willingham, John 21, 63, 97, 98
Willingham, Marge 98
Willingham's World Champion
      Barbecue River City Rooters 98
Willis, John 76

Y

Yazoo Delta Q 117
yellow fever 19
Yo Gotti (Mario Mims) 113
York, Joe 42
Youngblood, J.C. 109

ABOUT THE AUTHOR

Craig David Meek is a lifelong Memphian. He graduated from the University of Memphis with a degree in journalism and worked as a newspaper reporter, photographer and copy editor. He has owned a small wholesale automotive parts business for the past decade, making sales calls throughout the Mid-South. For the past three years, he has written about his quest to try all the barbecue and soul food restaurants in the Memphis area at his "Memphis Que" blog. He lives in the Vollentine-Evergreen neighborhood with his wife, Jessica Elvert, their border collie and their two gray tabby cats.